Rugs to Riches

Rugs to Riches

AN INSIDER'S GUIDE

TO ORIENTAL RUGS

Caroline Bosly

PANTHEON BOOKS / NEW YORK

Hardcover edition originally published by Pantheon Books, a division of
Random House, Inc. in 1980.

Grateful acknowledgment is made to the following for
permission to reproduce previously published material:

Doris Leslie Blau, Inc., for photograph of Savonnerie rug.

Murray L. Eiland for photograph from Chinese and Exotic
Rugs. *Courtesy Murray L. Eiland.*

Fabio Formenton for photograph from Rugs and Carpets of
the Orient *by Nathaniel Harris. Archivio Arnoldo Mondadori*
Editore, Milan.

Mohamed Seyed Ghaleh for photographs and prose excerpt from
The Romance of Persian Carpets, *Cyrus-Verlag, Celle, West Germany.*

Holle Verlag GmbH for photograph from Oriental Rugs and
Carpets *by Fabio Formenton, 1972.*

Office du Livre, Fribourg, Switzerland, and Charles E. Tuttle
Company, Inc., Rutland, Vermont, for photographs from
Connoisseur's Guide to Oriental Carpets *by E. Gans-Ruedin.*

Routledge & Kegan Paul Ltd. for photographs from A View
of Chinese Rugs *by H. A. Lorentz, 1972.*

Library of Congress Cataloging in Publication Data
Bosly, Caroline.
Rugs to riches.
Bibliography: p.
Includes index.
1. Rugs, Oriental. I. Title.
NK2808.B764 746.7' 5' 075 80-7704
ISBN 0-394-50039-3
0-394-73957-4

Book design by Elissa Ichiyasu
Maps and drawings by Susan Gaber

Manufactured in the United States of America
9

CONTENTS

ACKNOWLEDGMENTS

I appreciate the loving support and consistent encouragement given to me by my parents, Cynthia Wibmer and Martin Denzil Wibmer.

I would like to thank Kai Vickers and David Wilkins for their support, together with my friends and colleagues in the international bonded warehouses. My thanks also to all my clients, who gave me encouragement and many of whom took the time to fill in my questionnaire.

The following people generously gave me the benefit of their expert knowledge: Doris Blau, retail rug markets; J. V. Bosly, rug auctions; Dimitri Georgitis, Greek scholarship; Jack Izmidlian, bibliographer; Phillip Morris and R. Behar, rug restoration; Ted Skilford, interior design; and Dr. Alan N. Schoonmaker, concepts of negotiating.

For their diligence, patience, energetic research, and sheer hard work, my heartfelt thanks to Peggyann Chevalier, Inez Mackenzie, Sarajane Mackenzie, Bunty Robinson, and Alden Rockwell.

My special thanks to Mohamed Seyed Ghaleh for all his wonderful photographs, and to Karin Schulze for her expert help in selecting them. I am also grateful to Edward Minassian for his drawings which he so kindly gave me, and to Michael Stanway, who photographed the Hereke rugs and the "Kennedy" rug.

My warm thanks must also go to Barbara Plumb and her assistant, Robin Stevens, and to R. D. Scudellari and his assistant, Elissa Ichiyasu, for their help in the presentation of my book.

Finally, I offer my appreciation to all the weavers, dye masters, designers, and others who create these magic carpets.

CAROLINE BOSLY

To F.T.M.,
without whom this book would
never have been written

The roof tops of Qum.

CHAPTER ONE

Setting the Scene

I have been a broker to the world market of oriental rugs for many years and I want you to be an insider before you buy your next oriental rug. As a broker, my job is to know just which rugs are where at any given time. I take private buyers around the bonded warehouses where the rugs are stored before being redistributed around the world. This helps my clients to find the one rug that will be just right for their homes and it also helps me to keep up to date with the constantly changing stocks.

In the course of guiding private buyers through these modern-day Aladdin's caves, I have been asked many questions which my clients tell me they have been unable to find the answers to in books currently available: How do I know if a rug is a genuine oriental and not just a machine-made copy? What do the colors and patterns symbolize? Which oriental rugs make the best investments? Can I really use my rug or is it too precious? What do I do if red wine is spilled on my new rug?

This is why I have written *Rugs to Riches*. I hope it will help to answer these questions and clear up some of the mysteries so that your path may be smooth as you begin to explore this intriguing world.

I have deliberately tried to keep this book fairly short. A pet peeve of mine is "guide" books that weigh me down whenever I carry them around to guide me. I felt I should spend my space giving you inside information, things that you really *do* need to know, to guide you in the world of oriental rugs.

OVERVIEW

Rugs to Riches will describe how oriental rugs are made and tell you how to know whether or not a rug is handmade and in which country it was made—sometimes even which town or village. I will explore the meanings of colors and designs so that you can "read" a rug and understand its meaning. You will learn how to judge a rug for its quality and value and estimate its price before you buy so that you will know whether or not the store is being fair to you.

There is a chapter on first aid—small repairs that you can do at home that will save you money and save many rugs from fraying away. In the same chapter you will find tips for coping with accidents that may happen as you use your rug. There are ideas for decorating with rugs so that your investment need not always be under your feet; and in another chapter I tell you which rugs I feel will make the best investments as your personal hedge against inflation.

By reading this book, you will gain an understanding of the "antique" rug market—what to look for and how to grow your own antiques. There is a chapter on how to bargain at your local store for the rug you want, which will also save you money. And finally, I will describe different ways of collecting rugs and of auctioning and selling them, if and when you should want to do so.

As you can see, this book is not only to read but to *use*, over and over again. In the beginning, you may find its benefit is in the knowledge you've gained. Later, its value may be more in the area of the skills it has helped you to develop. The book's ultimate usefulness may be in the money it has saved you and in the pleasure your rugs will give you.

THE HERITAGE OF RUGS

Weaving is one of the most ancient crafts in the world. It is mentioned in the Old Testament and in Homer's *Iliad*. Documents about weaving exist from the period of the Sassanid Dynasty, which ruled Persia from the third century to the middle of the seventh century. Woolen carpets woven in Persia are referred to in the Chinese Sui Annals (A.D.590–617). And who can forget Cleopatra's famous encounter with Caesar, arriving at his feet rolled up in an oriental carpet?

The oldest surviving rug is the Altai Rug. It was found in a mountainous region of southern Siberia, in the grave of a

Scythian warrior prince who died five hundred years before the birth of Christ. The prince was buried in a mound according to the custom of his day, together with enough possessions to ensure that his life in the next world would be a comfortable one. Grave robbers soon disturbed the grave. They carried away the metal objects and precious stones but ignored the rug as they ran off, leaving the entrance to the burial chamber open on their way out. During the next heavy rains, water flooded the grave; the water turned to ice and the rug was "deep-frozen." It was found, well preserved, by the Russian archaeologist S. I. Rudenko, who was exploring in the region in 1947–1949. The Altai Rug is also known as the Pazyryk Rug, as that is the name of the valley in which it was discovered. It is now on view in the Hermitage Museum in Leningrad.

The Altai Rug has a terra-cotta-colored central field with the design woven in pale blues, beiges and yellows. The pattern is surprisingly modernistic: small squares filled with simple stylized flowers. The innermost of the five main borders contains octagons closely resembling the octagons, or *guls*, of later Turkoman weaving; the second border portrays processions of lifelike elks; the third border is a repeat of the stylized flowers shown in the central field. The Scythians buried seven horses with each chief and the fourth major border of the Altai shows processions of seven horsemen on each side. The rug is almost square—six by six and a half feet (1.83 × 1.98 m.). It is tied with the Turkish Ghiordes knot (which I will describe later) and has 200 knots to the square inch.

Precisely where the Altai Rug was woven will probably never be decided. One opinion is that it was made in Persia. However, the Persian border is nearly two thousand miles (3,218 km.) southwest of where the rug was found. It seems more logical that the Altai Rug was woven by the Scythians themselves. The Scythians were migrants from the Mongolian region and the Mongol artists frequently depicted animals in their designs, which was unusual at that time in Persia.

The earliest beginnings of rug-weaving in Mongolia, China and Tibet are unknown. What evidence there is seems to indicate that the art of knotting rugs was introduced from Mongolia into China and from China into Tibet. It is believed that some Mongol designs found their way into Asia after the Mongol conquest at the beginning of the thirteenth century. By the middle of the eighteenth century, Mongol rugs had basically become Chinese in nature, although they never equaled the restrained elegance of the Chinese ones.

Tibetan rugs, on the other hand, have always been funda-

The Altai Rug, also known as the Pazyryk Rug, circa 500 B.C.

mentally Chinese, with the addition of some Tibetan symbols and brighter colors.

The first Chinese rugs were probably just embroidered felt, and rare examples of eighth-century felt rugs are in the museum at Nara in Japan. Because of China's isolation from the rest of the world, the history of Chinese rugs is obscure. All the experts seem to disagree as to the amount of influence the Near East had on rug-making in China and vice versa. Perhaps both areas influenced each other. One thing is definite, however: once you have seen even a few classical nineteenth-century Chinese rugs, you will find that they are easily distinguishable from every other type of oriental rug. Antique Chinese rugs were always woven in subtly blended *complementary* colors. Very few colors (sometimes only two) were included in any single rug, but every *tone* of those colors was used to give the rugs their quiet grandeur. The designs of Chinese rugs are unique (see Chapter 4) and, in contrast to all other rugs, the incredible clearness of the design details does not depend on the fineness of the knotting. Again in contrast to rugs from other countries, classical Chinese rugs do not differ from one area to another. Two rugs that were woven thousands of miles apart look so similar that, instead of being named after the area, they were generally named after the dynasties or emperors who were in power at the time.

618–906   T'ang Dynasty
The flowering of artistic talent; felt rugs were used as floor coverings.

907–960   Five Dynasties
China's "Dark Ages."

960–1279   Sung Dynasty
Art was at its highest point; 1206, Genghis Khan became leader of the Mongols; 1262, the first reference to Mongol rug workshops.

1280–1368   Mongol Yüan Dynasty
Kublai Khan (grandson of Genghis Khan) ruled; Marco Polo was at the khan's court for many years; China and Persia exchanged weavers.

1368–1644   Ming Dynasty
The oldest preserved Chinese knotted rugs date from the end of this dynasty.

1644–1912   Ch'ing Dynasty, emperors
1644 1661   Shun Chih: light blue introduced.
1662–1722   K'ang Hsi: floral designs introduced, geometric designs declined; more use of colors and patterns.
1723–1735   Yung Cheng.
1736–1795   Ch'ien Lung: colors refined, more grace, subtlety, balanced composition.
1796–1820   Chia Ch'ing: beginning of major decline.
1821–1850   Tao Kuang: rugs copied from earlier centuries.
1851–1861   Hsien Feng: Empress Dowager ruled both directly and indirectly a quarter of the world's population for fifty-three years (1856–1908).
1862–1874   T'ung Chih: rugs copied from earlier centuries.
1875–1908   Kuang Hsü: rugs copied from earlier centuries.
1908–1912   Hsüan T'ung: revolution, 1911; republic formed, 1912.

To celebrate his defeat of the Romans and his conquest of southern Arabia, the Persian king Chosroes I (A.D.531–579) ordered a very special carpet to be made for his palace at Ctesiphon. This rug was known as the Spring Carpet of Chosroes and was the most expensive carpet ever made. It was probably a flat-woven piece (as contrasted with a pile carpet), and some scholars estimate that it may have measured as much as four hundred feet long by almost one hundred feet wide (121.8 ×

30.5 m.) and they calculate it to have weighed more than two tons. Unfortunately, we cannot know for certain because in 627, King Chosroes II was defeated by the Byzantine emperor Heraclius, who did not appreciate the carpet. Heraclius allowed visitors to his court to cut pieces from the rug and take them home as souvenirs. However, the *garden* design is still woven today, albeit in a much simplified form.

The Spring Carpet of Chosroes was said to have been brocaded with gold and silver and studded with precious jewels. The design was that of an enormous garden, with trees, paths, streams and flower beds highlighted with silk. The idea was that the king should feel that he was in a garden no matter what the season—whenever he contemplated the carpet it would always seem like spring. Chosroes' carpet was so large that the king could actually stroll down its woven paths and stand beside its woven flower beds.

Both Christians and Moslems associate beautiful gardens with the word "paradise." The Persian poet Sadi described a garden as "a carpet spread by the night winds in the shadow of the trees." So much of Persia is made up of barren mountains and deserts that it is understandable that gardens filled with flowers and streams would seem like paradise to the people of that country. "Lovely songs in the garden, clear water in the meadow, this filled with colorful tulips and that full of fruits without number. Rustling through the shady hall of trees, the winds make a shimmering carpet." This verse appears on a Persian carpet made in the sixteenth century. It is a garden carpet filled with brightly colored flowers and singing birds. It was only in the sixteenth century that Persian weavers were able to weave garden carpets equal in beauty to the Spring Carpet of Chosroes.

When Marco Polo was traveling in the East in the thirteenth century, he named Konya in Turkey as the town where "the most beautiful carpets in the world," as he described them, were woven. It is thought that these rugs were woven by Armenians and Greeks living in Turkey at the time. Regardless of the nationalities of these weavers, the influence of the Islamic culture can be clearly seen in the development of oriental rugs.

The Islamic religion was certainly responsible for the creation of the most frequently appearing type of all oriental rugs—the prayer rug. The Koran requires that the faithful wash, find a clean place and prostrate themselves on the ground, facing towards Mecca to say their prayers five times each day. A small rug is obviously the perfect solution for this; it is easy both to keep clean and to carry about. Consequently hundreds of thousands of prayer rugs have been made throughout the centuries.

The Crusaders of the eleventh century brought many varieties of rugs back with them from the Middle East and were probably responsible for introducing rugs to Europe. The written records of this period are unclear but through the medium of painting we have proof that oriental rugs were used in Europe. By the end of the fourteenth century, Italian artists had become sufficiently aware of oriental rugs to use them in their paintings. In the fifteenth century, Van Eyck, Memling and other famous Flemish artists often used rugs to give interest and color to the background settings of their portraits of the prosperous middle class. The artists' realistic and detailed style allows us to recognize the mainly Turkish rugs they chose to paint.

Many famous persons also had their portraits painted in a setting of oriental rugs. At Welbeck Abbey in England there is a portrait of Queen Elizabeth I (1533–1603) in the garden of Wanstead. At her feet lies the Sword of State and her little dog is sitting beside it. And spread on the grass beneath her, perfectly complementing her white dress with its embroidery of sprays of flowers in natural colors, is one of Lord Leicester's oriental carpets.

Hans Holbein the Younger used rugs so often in the backgrounds of his paintings that the glowing red Turkish Bergamas he chose have come to be known as Holbein rugs. King Henry VIII had several of his portraits painted with these "princely" rugs appearing in the background. He was among the first in England to import large numbers of oriental rugs, some of which exist today in the royal collection.

A famous Persian rug now in the Victoria and Albert Museum in London is the Ardebil Rug. This rug is one of a pair that was bought by a firm of European dealers in the late 1880s. In 1893 the Victoria and Albert Museum bought the carpet for about $4,000. In those days that was an excessively high price to pay for a rug. The museum thought it was even more excessive when they became aware that large areas of their rug had been damaged and subsequently had been replaced by parts taken from the second rug in the Ardebil pair (which is now in the Los Angeles County Museum of Art).

The Ardebil Rug measures thirty–four and a half feet by seventeen and a half feet (10.52 × 5.33 m.) and its knot count varies between 297 and 324. It is made of wool, woven onto silk warp and weft threads. The design is a circular yellow medallion on a deep sapphire blue ground. The rug bears a woven inscription, translated by Rexford Stead, formerly of the Los Angeles County Museum of Art, which reads: "Except for thy haven, there is no refuge for me in this world; other than here,

The Ardebil Rug, circa 1540.

there is no place for my head. The work of a servant of the Court, Maqsud of Kashan, 946." The Moslem date of 946 is approximately equivalent to 1540 in our dating system.

Oriental rug scholars disagree as to whether the Ardebil rugs were originally made for the mosque at Ardebil or for the mosque of Imam Riza in Meshed. As these carpets were made over four hundred years ago, it is unlikely that their exact histories will ever be known. What is important, however, is that the finely detailed work of Maqsud is still available to us to enjoy today.

In Europe at the end of the sixteenth century, oriental rugs and carpets were rare, fabulously expensive and becoming enormously popular among the richest and most powerful families, who were the only ones able to afford them. The constant outpouring of money to buy these rugs was putting a strain on the national purse strings. In order to solve this problem, in 1608 France's King Henry IV (1553–1610) instructed Pierre Dupont, who had a considerable knowledge of weaving, to begin organizing the production of "oriental" rugs to be woven within the borders of France. (Dupont had personally perfected a rug called "à la façon de Perse et du Levant," the quality of which was judged to be equal to that of fine Turkish pieces.) King Henry ordered that an atelier (factory or workshop) be set up inside the palace of the Louvre. The venture was to be sponsored by the king.

These early carpets were made of wool with a Turkish-style knot and they were sheared so that the pile had a velvety appearance. Notable artists were commissioned and they created floral designs in the style of contemporary French decorative art. However, apart from encouraging native craftsmanship, Henry's venture into the world of commerce rather defeated its own purpose. He was so delighted by the first completed rug that he decreed that henceforth all rugs and carpets made in the Louvre would be for the exclusive use of the royal family (although he is reported to have sent one fine example to the shah of Persia). The output of the atelier was rather limited. Even the most practiced weavers only managed to knot at one-tenth the rate usual in the Orient (a situation which remains true to this day).

King Henry IV died abruptly in 1610 but the atelier continued to flourish at the Louvre. When Louis XIII (1601–1643) grew up (he was only nine years old when he came to the throne) he, too, took an interest in the weaving of the "French orientals." Irritated by their limited production at the Louvre, in 1627 he ordered Dupont to establish a second atelier. This Dupont did with the help of one of his former pupils, Simon Lourdet. The second atelier, of which Dupont appointed Lourdet director, was founded on the banks of the Seine at Chaillot, an outlying district of Paris. The building that they converted had been a children's home named Hospice de la Savonnerie, which had been built on the site of a previous soap factory (*savon* means soap). The local people continued to refer to the building as La Savonnerie and

A Savonnerie carpet, late seventeenth century.

the carpets themselves soon came to be known as "Savonneries."
Savonneries were Europe's first original carpet design.

In 1672, during the long reign of Louis XIV, from 1643 to
1715, the original atelier was transferred from the Louvre and
combined with the one at Chaillot. Ninety large Savonneries
were ordered to furnish the great salons of the Louvre. Louis's

reign was almost over by the time this order was completed. The weavers were still slow and many of the carpets were to be as much as thirty feet long by sixteen feet wide (9.30 × 4.88 m.). The leading court painter, Charles Lebrun, was appointed designer-in-chief. His work was in the elaborate baroque and later rococo styles, which were succeeded by Empire, neoclassical and eventually second baroque designs. To fully appreciate these Savonneries you need to see them in the palatial surroundings for which they were made. A magnificently harmonious effect was achieved by the coordination of the elaborate ceiling and wall patterns with the floor coverings.

By 1743, the edict that Savonneries were to be reserved for the exclusive use of the royal family had been lifted—not, however, before a law to protect the royal investment had been made. This law prohibited the importation into France of any oriental rugs or carpets. Consequently, because the Savonneries were so expensive and in order to fill the popular demand for rugs, the Aubusson factory was started. This produced rugs woven in the style of a tapestry. They were made in a heavier quality than was usual in tapestry-weaving, so despite the fact that Aubussons had no pile to protect their foundation threads and thus were rather delicate, they were sufficiently practical to be used as decorative floor coverings. Although they lacked a pile and consequently were not very warm, they could be made quite quickly and were relatively affordable. The colorings and designs followed those of the Savonnerie rugs but the sizes of the Aubusson rugs were much smaller. They were intended for use in the small *appartements* that were so popular in Paris in the late eighteenth and nineteenth centuries.

Because of the considerable trading that took place between Turkey and Europe, the majority of rugs that came to Europe were of Turkish origin. It was not until the seventeenth century that Persian rugs began to be imported in any great numbers. One of my ancestors, Sir Anthony Sherley (1565–1635), was responsible for the first major consignment of Persian rugs that was intended to be delivered to England. Sir Anthony was an English adventurer who found himself appointed ambassador to Persia in 1599. He became friendly with Shah Abbas I, also known as Shah Abbas the Great (1587–1628), and the shah soon assigned him the task of arranging an anti-Turkish pact between the principal European powers and Persia. A large number of Persia's finest rugs were to be sent to Europe (as well as thirty-two crates of other fabulous presents) in the care of Sir Anthony as proof of Persia's good intentions, great wealth and superior craftsmanship. While the Venetian merchants trading with the

Levant (now Turkey) were busy importing Turkish rugs, Persian weavers were producing some of the finest pieces ever made. We don't know exactly how many of these superb rugs Shah Abbas gathered together for the consignment but the number is said to have been "several hundred pieces." Unfortunately, none of them ever made it to Europe. Sir Anthony returned, alive but poor, and without his consignment. There is no record of what happened to several hundred of possibly the finest rugs Persia had ever produced.

In spite of Sir Anthony's misfortunes, contacts between Europe and Persia became more frequent. Persia and Poland became particularly friendly. Persian weavers were sent to Poland to teach the Poles how to weave and, therefore, to create a new Polish industry. The venture was unsuccessful and, contrary to popular belief, the famous Polonaise rugs were not made in Poland but in the town of Isfahan in Persia. The Polonaise rugs took their name from the great Polish families who commissioned them. The weavers were frequently ordered to incorporate Polish coats of arms into the designs of the rugs. Polonaise rugs were often woven in silk, with gold and silver brocade adding to their splendor. The traditional bright colors of Persia were softened to accord with the European preference for pastel shades of lemon, lime and apricot, and the intricate detail of Persia's designs was simplified to become sweeping patterns of flowers.

It was in the late seventeenth century that oriental rugs were brought to America by the wealthy English families who moved to the colonies. As the colonies grew and became established towns, and cabins became houses and mansions, the earlier settlers wanted appropriate floor coverings like the ones the English brought with them. Virginia was the first and foremost importer of oriental rugs and soon the ships that sailed from England to America began to carry rugs as a regular part of their cargo.

Throughout the eighteenth and nineteenth centuries and into the twentieth century, oriental rugs were to be found in most of the well-to-do homes in America. There they remained until, with the advent of machine-made rugs and the first wall-to-wall carpeting, orientals were suddenly passé. The fact that machine-made carpets wore out more quickly was unimportant; they were inexpensive and could easily be replaced. So thousands of old and neglected oriental rugs were simply tossed into the dustbins. However, a few people did recognize their value: the Armenian and other dealers in rugs had the foresight to gather up the discarded rugs (I personally know of five fortunes that were built by rescuing these "worthless" rugs).

America's only indigenous "oriental" rugs are made by American Indians, mostly by the Navajo tribes. In the sixteenth century, the Navajos settled in what is now south-central Colorado and northern New Mexico, where they were taught how to weave by the Pueblo Indians. For the next two hundred years, the Navajos made blankets, clothing and floor coverings in simple striped patterns and soft natural colors. Then gradually, throughout the nineteenth century, the style of the Navajos' weaving began to change as they were influenced by contact with the white man. Diamond and zigzag patterns were introduced into the rugs. In the 1880s, the railroads brought machine-spun, aniline-dyed wools to the Navajos; they also brought tourists who willingly bought the Navajos' weavings, especially their rugs, in great numbers. At this time the "oriental" look was very much in vogue, so that any design that looked oriental was encouraged and the Navajos were even given patterns to follow.

By 1890, most Navajo rugs were being woven solely for commercial reasons. These rugs were gaudy and loosely woven into bold patterns. Just as the advent of the railroads had helped to destroy the original style of the Navajos' weaving, so at the beginning of this century it was Fred Harvey, the owner of a railroad company, who helped to re-establish their natural artistry. He encouraged the Navajos to return to their traditional methods of weaving, using hand-spun yarns and natural colors. These days, although most of the rugs are made using machine-spun wools chemically dyed in bright colors, at least there are still a few Navajos weaving rugs in the traditional way.

The central market for oriental rugs is situated in the unlikely place of London, England. Until the turn of this century most of the influential oriental rug families had centered their trade in Istanbul, but because of major political upsets in Turkey at that time the merchants moved to London and were granted a free port zone. London has been the central collecting point for rugs ever since.

Rugs from Iran, Turkey, China, Pakistan, Afghanistan, India, Africa, Eastern Europe and Peru are now sent to London, to huge bonded warehouses where they are sorted and graded. Ninety-seven percent of them are re-exported all over the world. In many countries government subsidies make rugs cheaper for the export market than for use in the home country, encouraging their exportation and yielding valuable foreign exchange. (Nevertheless, many rugs find their way back to the very country in which they were made, bought by individuals, dealers and museums.)

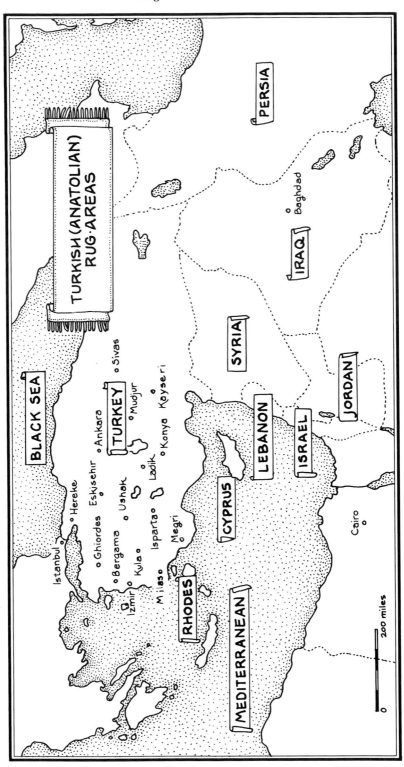

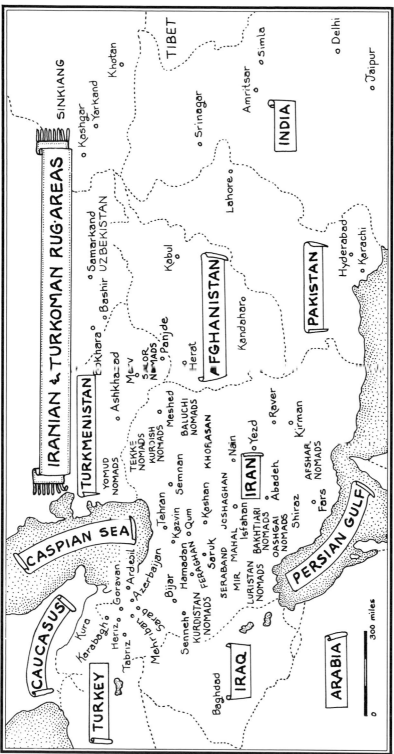

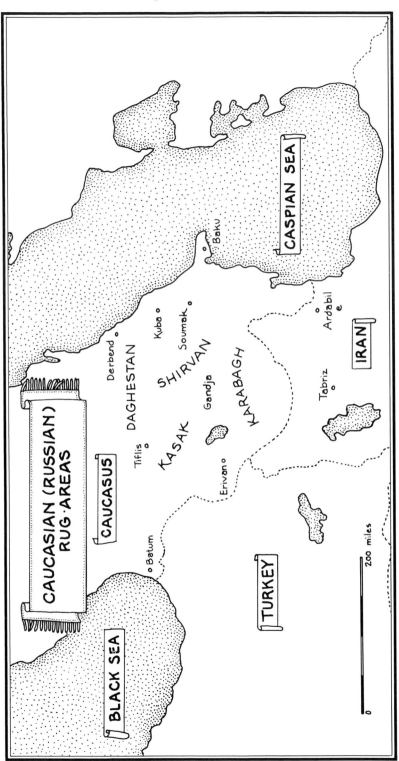

CAUCASIAN (RUSSIAN) RUG·AREAS

CAUCASUS

BLACK SEA

CASPIAN SEA

IRAN

TURKEY

Batum

Tiflis

Derbend

Kuba

Soumak

Baku

SHIRVAN

DAGHESTAN

KASAK

Gandja

KARABAGH

Erivan

Tabriz

Ardabil

200 miles

0

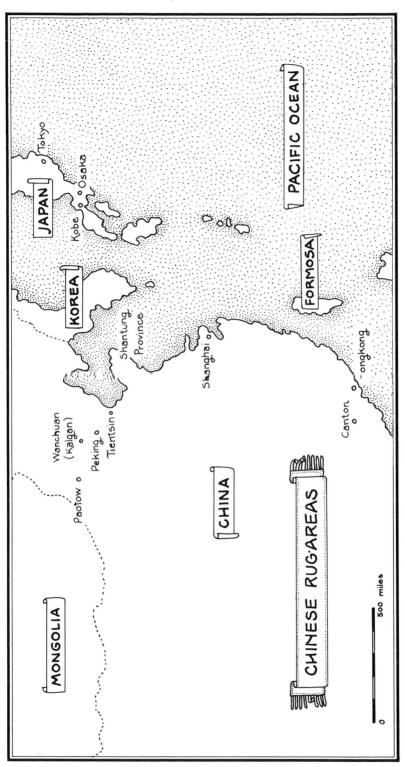

Along with the benefit of government subsidies, buyers can take advantage of the fact that they can choose a wide variety of rugs at the same time and in the same place and can ship them all together to their stores in Istanbul, Teheran, Delhi, Hamburg or New York, or wherever their businesses happen to be.

Spinning the yarn.

CHAPTER TWO

Untying the Knot

Wﾟhen oriental rugs are mentioned in the West some people, whose personal experience of rugs is limited to the ones they have seen in the homes of their grandparents, may tend to imagine three things: the color red, busy designs and extremely high prices. All of these things may be true, although none of them need be. Somewhere there exists your idea of the perfect rug; the only problem is knowing what to look for and where to find it. This is complicated by the fact that the choice is endless because oriental rugs are made in every color, design and quality imaginable.

Many eminent authorities have written many volumes about oriental rugs; however, it is basically a simple subject. I believe it is time to return to the first principles of what is, after all, a peasant handicraft.

The classic rule that a collector of oriental rugs must insist on is: every piece (that's how we describe rugs in the trade) must be *entirely handmade*. It is only the handmade orientals that will give endless joy, appreciate in value and outlast their machine-made cousins by fifty years or more. Machine-made rugs are not what is understood by the term "orientals" no matter what the salesman says and no matter where the rugs have been made. A machine-made rug is meant for use simply as a floor covering. When compared with the true oriental, it lacks charm, originality, durability and investment value. The machine-made copy may initially cost you less—or seem to—

but pause to consider its replacement cost after, for instance, ten years of family life. Add to this the cost of inflation and the fact that the rug has little, if any, resale value. Then you may wish you had spent a relatively small extra amount of money and bought an original handmade oriental rug. A true oriental at ten years old would still be considered new by the trade, and if you did want to sell it, it should show you a handsome profit.

A quick test to see if a rug is handmade is to turn it upside down and look at the back. If you cannot see the pattern as clearly as on the face, the rug is not handmade. If the rug passes this first test, bend it back on itself to expose the roots of the pile. If you can see rows of knots at the base of the tufts, the rug is handmade. But if the strands of wool are simply looped around the foundation threads, so that they can be pulled out with a pair of tweezers, the rug is machine-made.

These tests will also give you an indication of the quality of the rug. The more distinctly the design shows on the back, the greater the number of knots and the better the quality of the rug. In other words, the greater the number of hand-tied knots per square inch, the finer the piece: 150 knots per square inch is average; "fine" rugs may have a knot count of 500 or more. The highest knot count that I know of was found in a modern Persian Isfahan which had a staggering 1,200 knots in one square inch. So when choosing your rug, always be sure to look at the back to see how it is made before you fall in love with its pretty face.

Left: The front of a Hereke prayer rug. Right: The back, almost indistinguishable, which is as it should be.

Each dot represents one hand-tied knot. The first drawing shows 100 knots per square inch; the second, 300 knots per square inch; and the third, 600 knots per square inch.

Although I will be discussing many different types and styles of rugs, the one thing they all have in common is that they are all one hundred percent handmade.

Oriental rugs are made in many countries besides Persia, or Iran, as the country is called today. The Turkish people, too, have been weaving rugs for more than a thousand years. Fine rugs are made in Afghanistan, Pakistan, India and China, as well as in Greece, Bulgaria, Romania and Russia. Especially famous are the rugs from the Turkoman and Caucasian regions of the Soviet Union. Egypt produces handmade rugs and some are also made in the Americas and North Africa. The general definitions that I will give you in this chapter are true for all the handmade rugs that are termed oriental rugs which depict the artistry, history and dreams of their creators, whether they are made in Persia or Peru or anywhere in between.

HOW RUGS ARE MADE

All of these geographically distant weavers use similar methods to make their rugs. Weaving is a relatively simple craft, requiring long hours of work but only a few relatively inexpensive materials. Therefore, it is a craft often practiced by the poorer peasant communities and nomadic tribes. It is largely considered to be woman's work, convenient to do at home along with the household chores. Children, when they are two or three years old, help by making a game of collecting the strands of wool; by the time they are seven or eight, they will have very naturally learned the process of weaving from their mother. While men are sometimes employed in town-centered workshops, rarely will the men of a village or tribe allow themselves to become involved in the actual weaving of the rugs, although they will help with the building of the looms and with the gathering of the materials and various dye stuffs.

All oriental rugs are regarded as being "woven" even though their designs are created by knotting. Weaving refers to the fact that the rugs are made on looms and has nothing to do with whether a rug is actually woven or knotted. There are two basic types of looms on which oriental rugs are made; one is vertical and the other is horizontal. The vertical loom is permanent and is used in towns and villages. The horizontal loom is used by the nomadic tribes because it can be easily taken apart and transported on the backs of pack animals when the tribe moves on.

Although weavers of the towns and villages both use the same style of vertical permanent looms, the town looms are usually larger, whether they are in workshops or in someone's home. Vertical looms are solidly constructed because they will be used to make many rugs and so are expected to last for a long time. This type of loom consists of two vertical posts connected by two strong cross beams, resulting in a very sturdy frame. The cross beams are adjustable so that the weaving of different sizes of rugs is possible. A workshop loom may be as high as twenty feet (6.09 m.) and equally wide. Facing the loom is a narrow bench on which the weavers sit side by side. As the rug progresses, either this bench can be raised until the weavers are almost bumping their heads on the ceiling, or the warp may be slackened so that the completed part of the rug can be wound around the bottom beam and the weavers can then work at a convenient level.

The first step in weaving a rug is to wind parallel vertical threads into place between the cross beams on the loom. These are called the *warp*. They are set close together; the fineness of the eventual rug depends in part on the closeness of these threads. You will see the warp appearing as the fringes at either end of the finished rug. It is possible for the warp threads to be made of silk or even wool, but they are usually made of cotton because it is less expensive than silk and stronger than wool. If a warp bar is used, the warp is still strung vertically between the two cross beams but then it is looped around a third, thin pole placed horizontally across the warp. When the weaver has completed all the vertical warp threads, she is faced with something that looks rather like the strings of a harp.

The weaver next takes another long strand of cotton and weaves it horizontally in and out of alternate warp threads, from one edge of the rug to the other. The warp threads are held under tension by a flat rod which is used to divide the even-numbered threads (counting from left to right) from the odd-numbered threads. This separation is called the *shed*. The process of inserting lines of threads around alternating warps continues

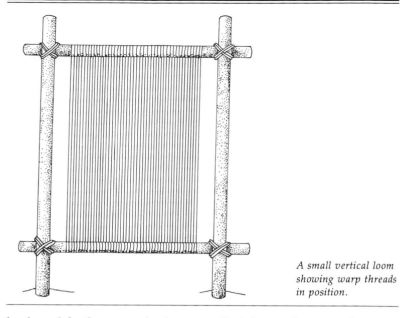

*A small vertical loom
showing warp threads
in position.*

back and forth across the loom until eight or nine strands are in place. These horizontal threads are called the *weft*. This simple technique forms a flat woven base that will later protect the rows of woolen knots from which the body of the rug will be formed. This base is called *kelim*, and it appears at the point where the fringe begins. Even a narrow kelim will prevent the knots from unraveling. It may be either plain or highly decorated, according to local custom and the whim of the weaver. Generally, town and village rugs have plain, undecorated kelim ends. On the other hand, the nomadic tribes prefer to make rugs with brightly colored, abstract designs on their kelim ends.

After approximately one to six inches (3 to 15 cm.) of kelim has been completed, the weaver ties her first row of knots. To tie a knot she will usually use only her fingers, but in some districts a knife with a hooked end is used to pull the ends of the wool out from between the warp threads. This knife is called a *tikh*. The blade of the knife is useful for cutting the wool after a knot has been tied. When the weaver has finished two or three rows of knots, she takes a long weft thread and once again weaves it in and out of the vertical warp threads. The weft is always hammered down onto the knots, for which a heavy iron, comblike tool, called a *daftun*, is used. This hammering down of the weft thread pushes the knots down very tightly and is one of the main reasons why oriental rugs are so strong. After the weft thread is hammered down, the weaver begins her next row of knots.

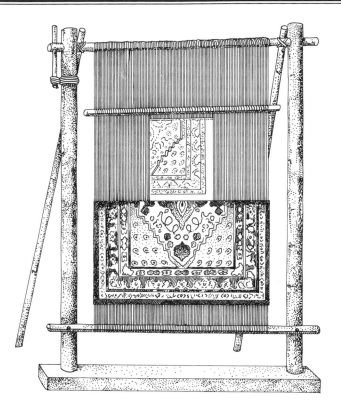

A vertical loom showing a partly finished rug together with the pattern the weaver will follow.

So, the loom has been constructed, the warp threads have been strung, an inch or more of the kelim has been woven and the first two or three rows of knots have been tied. The weft thread has been interwoven and hammered down, and the creation of an oriental rug is underway.

For the town and village rugs, the weaver will almost always follow a pattern drawn on graph paper. This pattern shows where each knot should be and what color it should be. Patterns of one kind or another have always been used to help create oriental rugs. Although nomadic weavers often create their own designs as they go along, they, too, will be following the general traditional designs of their tribe. In the towns and villages, artists design the patterns and dictate each of the colors for the rugs; the patterns are then sold in the bazaars.

Following her pattern (although I have never yet met a weaver who felt bound to follow exactly these predetermined designs and colors), the weaver chooses the appropriate wool from among the many different balls that hang conveniently on the loom. The outermost border of most oriental rugs is knotted in a solid color to provide a frame for the intricate central design. A skilled weaver takes only two or three seconds to tie each knot, then with her *tikh* she cuts the end of the wool to form tufts approximately four inches (10 cm.) long. The rug progresses in this way until there are five or six inches (13 or 15 cm.) of weaving on the loom. Because of the length of the tufts, it is difficult to see the design. So the weaver uses her *gaichi*—a type of scissors with a heavy guard along the upper blade—to trim the tufts until they are about two inches (5 cm.) long, and the beginnings of the design can be seen.

When the rug is finished, it is removed from the loom and the loose warp threads are left as loops, cut to form a straight fringe, or knotted into tassels. The two ends are often finished each in a different way, the one at the top being the more elaborate, and styles of finishing fringes vary widely from one region to another. After the fringe has been completed, the rug is then taken to the local master shearer, who will finely shave its entire face so that the design can, for the first time, be fully appreciated. This is a highly skilled profession. Keeping the length of the pile even is very difficult: one slip of the blade would spoil a rug that took months of laborious work to produce.

In the villages, the process of making a rug is basically the

Weavers at a workshop loom. Note sections of the pattern pinned to the warp threads above the partly woven rug, and also the daftun *lying on the bench.*

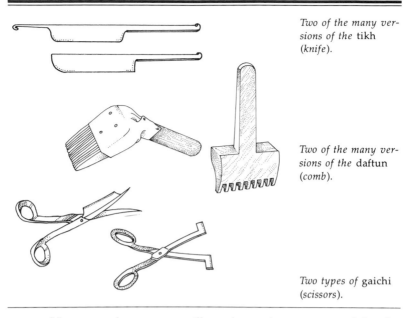

Two of the many versions of the tikh (knife).

Two of the many versions of the daftun (comb).

Two types of gaichi (scissors).

same. However, because a village loom is constructed in the weaver's home, it is, by necessity, much smaller than a town workshop loom. Village rugs are seldom larger than eight by five feet (2.44 × 1.52 m.); the average sizes are seven by four feet (2.13 × 1.22 m.), known as *dozar*, and five by three feet (1.52 × .91 m.), or *zaranim*. (A *zar* is approximately equivalent to one yard [.91 m.]: *dozar* means two zars and *zaranim* means one and a half zars.) It is possible to find pieces that measure nine by six (2.74 × 1.83 m.) or even ten by seven feet (3.05 × 2.13 m.), which of course indicates a larger home and more work space.

In Persia, when people refer to a *policheh* (meaning "rug") they actually mean a rug of about seven by four feet (2.13 × 1.22 m.), the dozar size, the size in which the majority of rugs are now made. So, if you're in a bazaar or store in Persia and ask to see "rugs," the dealer will only bring you rugs of the dozar size. If you want to see other sizes, you must ask for them specifically by size name. The tiniest rug, measuring three by two feet (.91 × .61 m.), is called a *pushti* (meaning "back"). These rugs are used to cover the cushions that line the walls of the reception area in Persian homes, so that people can rest their backs as they sit on the rug-strewn floor.

Until the nineteenth century, most Persian rugs were *keleys* (*keley* refers to the rug's size, about eight feet, six inches by five feet [2.59 × 1.52 m.], not its place of origin). In Persian homes, the reception room is usually built in a long thin shape. In Farsi, the language of Persia, *keley* means "head," and the traditional arrangement for the reception-room rugs was for the keley to be placed horizontally across one end of the room, with two wide runners (*kenarehs*) placed side by side and extending vertically from the keley down the length of the room. *Kenareh* means "side" or "banks of a river," a reference to water, a subject so important in a dry land.

From the beginning of the nineteenth century, rugs were woven in response to European demands. Because European rooms were usually square, the shapes of the oriental rugs were changed so that they could form centerpieces for these rooms. Large rugs became popular, especially the twelve-by-nine-foot (3.66 × 2.74 m.) and fourteen-by-ten-foot (4.27 × 3.05 m.) sizes.

However, oriental rugs are seldom made in exact predetermined sizes, so all that is possible is a general guide, which is as follows: three by two feet (.91 × .61 m.), five by three (1.52 × .91 m.), seven by four (2.13 × 1.22 m.), eight by five (2.44 × 1.52 m.), nine by six (2.74 × 1.83 m.), ten by seven (3.05 × 2.13 m.), eleven by eight (3.35 × 2.44 m.), twelve by nine (3.66 × 2.74 m.), fourteen by ten (4.27 × 3.05 m.) and sixteen by twelve (4.88 × 3.66 m.). There are larger pieces, of course, but as these have almost always been made to order for mosques or palaces or for the great houses of Europe, their sizes are not standardized.

There are also runners (or "strips," as the trade calls them). You can expect to find new runners in: eight by two feet, six inches (2.44 × .76 m.); nine by two feet, six inches (2.74 × .76 m.); ten by two feet, eight inches to three feet (3.05 × .81 to .91 m.); eleven by three feet (3.35 × .91 m); twelve by three feet, three inches (3.66 × .99 m.); thirteen by three feet, six inches (3.96 × 1.07 m.); fifteen by three feet, six inches (4.57 × 1.07 m.); and sixteen by four feet (4.88 × 1.22 m.).

The old or antique strips tend to be as wide as three feet, six inches (1.07 m.) or four feet, six inches (1.37 m.), regardless of whether they are eight feet (2.44 m.) long or sixteen feet (4.88 m.) long.

I am often asked what the difference is between an oriental rug and an oriental carpet. The answer is, simply, its size. Any piece that is forty square feet or less is described in the trade as a rug. For instance, an 8' × 5' (2.44 × 1.52 m.) piece is a rug while an 8'1" × 5' (2.47 × 1.52 m.) piece is a carpet. However, to avoid confusion with machine-made "carpeting," I have used the term "rug" throughout this book.

In general, the room-size carpets, measuring twelve by nine feet (3.66 × 2.74 m.) or larger, are made in the towns in *kar-hanehs*. *Kar-hanehs* (the Persian word for workshops) are often rather grandly referred to as factories, although they are nothing like the factories we think of. There is no trace of machinery, only lines of weavers at their looms and sometimes a *salim* (singer) who calls the knots and helps to give a rhythm to the weaving.

Each *kar-haneh* has a master knotter, who is by far the most important person there. This position is always held by a man. He has complete authority over his looms and is responsible for all the materials used. In the large workshops there are several master knotters, as it would be impossible for one man to properly control and supervise a dozen looms. However, a master knotter's authority over his three or four looms remains absolute. Occasionally he might put in a few knots in places where they are especially important to the design. He hires and fires the weavers and decides how much each one will be paid according to her skill. It has happened that a weaver who was fired by one master knotter was later rehired by another master knotter in the same workshop, as each unit is entirely independent.

Besides size, another difference between the *kar-haneh* rugs and the village rugs is the exactitude with which they are made. When you see a large, precise rug, usually densely knotted and with an elaborately flowing design, it will, with rare exceptions, have been made in a *kar-haneh*. These town rugs often have a knot count of 300 to 500 per square inch, with smooth circles incorporated into their designs. This allows the petals of a flower or the form of a small animal or bird to be drawn in a lifelike manner. And the variety of colors used in town rugs seems unlimited.

The smaller village rugs will also have beautiful and often complicated designs incorporating true circles. In general, however, village rugs are less precise and may have some small irregularities, either of shape or design. An average village rug will have a knot count of 120 to 300 per square inch, although any individual village may well produce much finer pieces. A wide variety of colors are used in village rugs but, mainly because of the economics of the situation, a single piece will be unlikely to contain more than six different colors. The town *kar-hanehs* have the advantage of being able to buy their materials in larger quantities and so at lower prices. This restriction on the village weavers only seems to increase their sensitivity to their choice of colors, and thus, some of the most artistically satisfying pieces have been produced in the villages.

The nomadic rugs are woven on a horizontal loom. This simple loom is basically just four pegs placed in the ground, with a cross beam at either end around which the warp threads are strung. The fact that the loom is easy to dismantle and

A nomadic family with their horizontal loom. The warp threads have been attached in preparation for weaving a rug.

transport is important to a nomad who will move on as his grazing flocks move on. The pegs of the loom are pulled up, with the warp and weft threads still attached, and the whole thing is rolled up and placed on the back of a pack animal. When the next campsite is found, the pegs are once again hammered firmly into the ground so that the two cross beams are held apart and the weaving can continue.

A nomad may have to dismantle the loom twenty times or more before a rug is completed. Because it is difficult to get exactly the same tension each time the loom is reassembled, nomadic rugs are often irregular in shape. They may be narrow at one end, or have a curving belly or a serpentine side. All this is perfectly acceptable, so long as the irregularities are not too extreme. Irregularities are considered to be part of the charm of nomadic rugs. The nomadic tribes usually weave small rugs, with the average size being zaranim, five by three feet (1.52 × .91 m.). Occasionally larger pieces are produced, but they always tend to be narrow because the two wooden beams of the loom must be light enough to be easily carried by the pack animal when the tribe is on the move; the wider the rug, the longer the cross beams must be and, consequently, the heavier they will be.

Nomadic rugs are usually made entirely of wool—warp and weft threads as well as the pile—so that when handled they feel quite limp compared with rugs woven on a sturdy cotton base. The nomadic woolen rugs are often bound at the outside edges with goat's hair or other animal hair which gives added protection

A group of nomads trekking to find fresh pasture for their flocks.

to the rugs' delicate edges. Occasionally, goat's hair will also be used for the warp threads.

Nomadic rugs are produced in a limited range of colors. The Baluchi tribe of the Iran-Afghanistan-border area, for example, will seldom use any colors other than dark reds and blues, although occasionally they incorporate shades of undyed cream-colored wool or camel's hair into their work. Other tribes use different color combinations according to their traditions and the availability of dye stuffs. However, it is rare to see a nomadic piece that is truly multicolored.

The knot count in tribal pieces is quite low—90 to 150 knots to the square inch—and the designs of these rugs will be very much simpler than those of rugs made in the towns or villages. The *prayer-arch* design is frequently used in its angular form. Also, you may find diamond-shaped medallions, sometimes surrounded by small stylized figures. Many of the designs have been passed down for countless generations and it is often impossible to interpret their abstract patterns, although they will have once had meaning. For a guide as to whether a particular rug was made by nomadic tribespeople, look closely at the design: since the nomads never learned to weave circles smoothly, all their designs will be angular. Nevertheless, they have a spontaneity and an originality that is all their own.

The decision to weave a village rug is made by the whole family, for it is a long and expensive process. The materials needed to weave even a very small rug, five by three feet (1.52 × .91 m.), may cost as much as the head of the household earns in a single month. The senior man of the family treks from his village to the nearest town. In the bazaar, he carefully seeks out a designer whose work pleases him. Although the area in which he lives will have its own traditional designs, for centuries it has been the practice for artists to refine designs and make them even more beautiful and sometimes to invent new ones. The designer will be well paid for his work. A new and intricate design that has never been used before will cost about 50,000 rials, or $700. To the unpracticed eye, there sometimes appears to be very little difference between this design and another. Nevertheless, it means that the possible price paid for the first rug woven in a new design will, if the rug is well made, be considerably higher. Perhaps it is a sort of one-upmanship.

Once the appropriate design has been found and the cost satisfactorily bargained over, the designer and the villager usually go together through the bazaar to select the wool, cotton and perhaps even silk if the rug is to be silk inlaid. Materials are often bought undyed. Again, there is vigorous bargaining over the price, and when this is concluded satisfactorily for all concerned, the next visit is to the dye maker where the exact shade of the colorings is discussed in detail. The process of dyeing the wools takes a long time (see Chapter 3). Once the wool is ready the villager returns home and begins constructing the loom. This is solidly built, and as I have explained, it must

A typical village in Persia.

A designer at work on an intricate design.

also be a convenient size so that the family can live comfortably in their home while the rug is being made. The weaving of a seven-by-four-foot (2.13 × 1.22 m.) rug, which may have 300 or more knots to the square inch, takes almost a year to complete.

After the construction of the loom the next step is the winding on of the warp threads. The weaver then begins to make the first small kelim end which, together with the fringes, will guard the ends of the rug. When the kelim is in place, the weaver may then begin her laborious work. With the design pinned to the loom, she follows it to the best of her ability; but she also improvises. For example, she may decide to make one small flower into a pair of flowers or perhaps add a butterfly to the design. It is these small changes that will give the rug its unique individuality and charm.

After the weaver has woven a few inches of rug, carefully inserting the warp threads and hammering them down with her *daftun,* the rug is ready for its initial clipping. Using her *gaichi,* she clips the face of the rug until the length of the pile is reduced from four or five inches (10 or 13 cm.) to approximately two inches (5 cm.) and the beautiful pattern can be seen for the first time. She then places another row of knots, another thread, another row of knots and so on, each time vigorously hammering down the warp threads onto the last row of knots so that the knots are held tightly in place, ensuring that the rug has a firm foundation. The work continues through the months until the day the knotting is finished. Then the end of the rug will have its other kelim end woven and finally the warp threads will be released from the loom and cut to form the fringes.

The rug now has to be cleaned, because by this time it is

quite dirty. It is dunked into the nearest river or stream and held under the water with heavy stones to prevent it from floating away. After the running water has cleaned it, the rug is laid out on the river bank to dry in the sunshine. If it is an especially fine rug, one that is made of silk or one with a high knot count such as 400 to 500 knots per square inch, the washing process is rather different. These rugs are taken to the nearest town where the master shearer washes them by hand.

After a rug has been cleaned, the master shearer shaves it with what looks very much like a straight-edge razor. The object of this nerve-racking exercise is to give a smooth, even finish to

A village weaver working at a vertical loom in her home.

Top: Newly made rugs being washed. Bottom: Rugs laid out to dry on the river bank.

the rug. When this process is over, the shearer often irons the pile as a finishing touch. This is done with a heavy old-fashioned smoothing iron and damp cotton cloths. This removes any wrinkles and also helps the rug to lie flat.

It is at this point that the difficult decision must be made as to whether to take the rug to the bazaar to sell or take it home and enjoy it for at least one season.

When a nomadic family wishes to weave a rug, the process is very much the same as for a village family, except that pretty much everything is do-it-yourself. The wool must be selected from the flocks and then it must be spun and carded. It is dyed with natural roots and substances which nomads can find around them, such as ochre, madder root, cochineal beetles, bark and berries. When the process of dyeing is finished, the loom is put together and the weaving can begin. The finished rug is washed when the tribe comes to a stream, and it becomes part of the family's possessions, keeping them warm in the wintertime and decorating their tent in the summertime.

MATERIALS

Rugs are made from five basic materials: wool, cotton, silk, jute and animal hair. These are used in various combinations, but the most frequent combination is of cotton warp and weft threads

The delicate process of shearing requires enormous concentration.

Ironing out the wrinkles.

*A nomad spinning
wool for her weaving.*

and woolen pile. Wool woven onto cotton is what you will most often find in rug stores.

The finest grade of wool, and by far the most expensive, is called *kurk*. Kurk wool costs approximately as much as silk; consequently, any rug woven from kurk wool is likely to be a top-quality piece. Kurk wool is often used in conjunction with a silk warp thread and sometimes the pile itself is inlaid with silk to highlight details of the design. The knot counts of rugs made with kurk wool average 450 knots per square inch and up, and the nap of these pieces tends to be clipped quite short. Kurk wool is shorn from the chest and shoulders of lambs who are just eight to thirteen months old. These lambs grow up in the high mountain districts and their wool feels like firm velvet—silky smooth yet springy.

Good-quality wool comes from well-cared-for sheep which, because they live in the higher, cooler regions, grow a full fleece to keep warm. The sheep are usually washed before being shorn once or twice during the summer months. Then the freshly sheared wool is washed again in water to which a small amount of lime has been added. This helps to free the wool of its impurities before it is combed, sorted and then spun by hand. It will always be spun into a single ply, or strand.

The poorest-quality wool, taken from dead sheep, is referred to as *tabachi*, "dead wool." An easy way to recognize a rug made from *tabachi* wool is to rub it with your hand. Notice how the wool feels. Good wool feels springy, while dead wool feels brittle and may actually break when you stroke it. In this case, you can expect the rug to deteriorate with even a moderate amount of wear. Excessive fluffing is also a sign of poor wool. You can test this by vigorously rubbing the pile in one direction for a minute or two to remove the loose fluff. Then repeat the process. Good wool seldom fluffs a second time and should definitely not fluff a third time. (The short-pile Persian pieces hardly fluff at all.) If you get the same amount of fluff the third time you rub the rug, the chances are that it has been made from dead wool bought very cheaply from the slaughterhouses.

Generally, good wool has a rather heavy, greasy feel to it, so a feeling of dryness and a lack of elasticity are bad signs. The exception to this rule is the Persian Senneh rugs, which feel dry and grainy (but they still don't fluff). The texture and sheen of wool varies considerably from one area to another partly due to the water the sheep drink. For instance, Afshar rugs (Persia) are quite soft and glossy whereas Tabriz rugs (Persia) are more wiry and have very little sheen. The sheen or glossiness of a woolen rug also depends to a large extent on how fine the pile is and whether it lies evenly or not, as with velvet. The reason that Pakistan rugs are so glossy is that, while they are still wet from being washed clean, they are "polished" with the sharp edge of a metal spade. The spade is scraped in the direction of the pile time and again to remove the excess fibers and give the rug a polished effect.

Silk, which originally came from China, is now being produced in Persia and Turkey as well. The finest silk comes from the first part of the amazingly long single thread with which the silkworm spins its cocoon. One strand can measure over five thousand feet (1,520 m.) in length. The more the cocoon is unraveled, the coarser the silk becomes until you get down to the slub silk (also known as Jap silk). This is made from the broken bits and pieces at the base of the cocoon. Slub silk is used only for inferior rugs, when it is often mixed with cotton. These rugs look coarse, and unless the material has been mercerized (chemically treated), they have almost no natural sheen—although they will still shine as long as they are ironed flat. Hanging in a shop window, a slub silk rug looks good, but its sheen lasts only until you shake it, walk on it or ruffle its surface.

Finding good silk rugs is more difficult than finding good woolen rugs, probably because they cost so much that stores hesitate to carry them in their inventory. Silk rugs are woven with a silk warp thread and have a weft thread made either of silk or fine cotton. The pile which forms the body of the rug should be made entirely of silk. Silk rugs are very beautiful and very precious but they are also much more delicate than wool rugs and should *never* be subjected to hard wear.

An "art silk" rug simply means one that is made entirely from mercerized cotton. Art silk is of course far less expensive

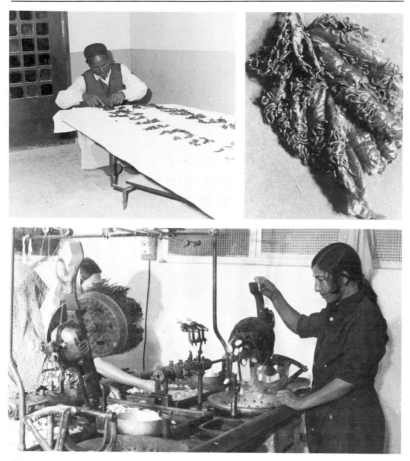

Silkworms are very carefully farmed. For the first seven days the young worms are fed shredded mulberry leaves (top left). For the second seven-day period, the worms are given whole leaves (top right). When they are fourteen days old, they graduate to leaves still attached to the twigs under which they will spin their cocoons when they are twenty-one days old. The silkworm takes three to four days to complete its cocoon. After the cocoons are gathered, they are immersed in boiling water to soften the gum that holds the filaments together. A device with revolving brushes (bottom) is submerged in the water, and the bristles catch up the loosened strands of silk.

than real silk, but although the mercerization process gives cotton a high gloss, the rug won't feel as smooth and it won't retain its glowing sheen in the way that real silk does. These mercerized rugs are woven with a natural cotton warp and weft thread and are most frequently found in Turkey. It is important to know whether you are buying a real silk rug or an art silk rug: the price difference can be as much as a thousand percent.

You can tell the difference between real silk and mercerized cotton by burning it. Silk is an animal substance and will smell like an animal if you burn enough of it. However, rather than trusting your nose, I suggest that you observe how a single strand burns. Pick out a strand from the back of the rug with a pin. It is wise to get the dealer's permission. Put the strand in an ashtray and light it with a match. Cotton, a vegetable substance, flares quickly, then burns down the strand, like paper or a small shaving of wood. Real silk is much more dramatic: the instant you light it, it flares, fuses, shrivels and rolls into a ball. This happens very quickly, so don't hold a strand between your fingers if you try it.

Real silk is also used in combination with wool and cotton and these pieces are referred to as being "silk-inlaid." In this case, the face of the rug will consist of wool pile with various features of the design woven in silk. For instance, the leaves and stem of a plant might be woven in wool and the flowers in silk. The warp and weft threads of silk-inlaid rugs are almost always cotton, which is less expensive than silk and gives the rugs a strong foundation. Because the surrounding wool protects the silk parts from heavy wear by spreading the load, silk-inlaid rugs are not nearly as delicate as pure silk ones. With a proper underlay (see Chapter 6) and given sensible care, a silk-inlaid rug is as suitable for use on the floor as a regular woolen one.

Jute, which tends to be brittle and easily broken, is only used in coarsely woven, inexpensive rugs, where it replaces cotton for the warp and weft threads.

Animal hair will be found mainly in nomadic rugs. It is sometimes mixed with sheep's wool for the weft threads, but more often you will find it being used to form the warp threads or the side cords of the rugs. Occasionally, a small amount of the fine hair of Kashmir and Angora goats is blended with wool to give it a special sparkle. Used by itself, goat's hair is unsuitable for weaving because the knots tend to work loose.

The wool of yaks is also used to make rugs. High in the Himalaya Mountains, in the land of the Abominable Snowman, the men of Tibet spin the wool and the women do the weaving. The wool is taken from the belly of the yaks and is spun, dyed and woven all within the small mountain villages. The yaks live on the main floor of the houses in the winter and the people live above them. In the summer, the animals roam outside. For a visitor, it is an unforgettable memory: the bright sun, the crisp air and the weathered faces of a group of men sitting on a stone wall, talking, laughing and spinning wool. Each wears one gold earring containing a large jewel which flashes in the sunlight. All this is framed against the awe-inspiring background of the highest mountain peaks in the world.

The finished rugs are loaded onto yaks which are adorned with brilliant red woolen earrings. This unique caravan slowly makes its way down the mountainside, accompanied by men carrying hay to feed the animals during the tedious journey. The precious cargo serpentines down thousands of feet on rocky trails and through rhododendron forests. At lower levels, the yaks may be replaced by donkeys or, in some instances, the men themselves may carry the loads for the final trip to the bazaars in the valleys. Some caravans travel all the way to Nepal and the fascinating city of Kathmandu to sell their rugs. The journey takes three weeks in each direction.

The Tibetan weavers love bright colors and use blues, yellows and reds in cheerful combinations. Their woolen rugs are woven onto either cotton or woolen foundation threads and they are quite coarsely knotted.

TYPES OF KNOTS

The two principal types of knots that are used in rug-making are the *Persian Senneh* knot and the *Turkish Ghiordes* knot. The Senneh knot is a single knot. It is made by passing the woolen strand under one warp, then over and around the next, so that the two ends of the pile show on either side of each warp thread. This knot can be made to face to the left or right so that the lie of the pile can be in either direction.

The Ghiordes knot is a double knot. It is made by looping the knot around two warp threads and bringing both ends of the wool out between them. The Turkish Ghiordes knot gives a

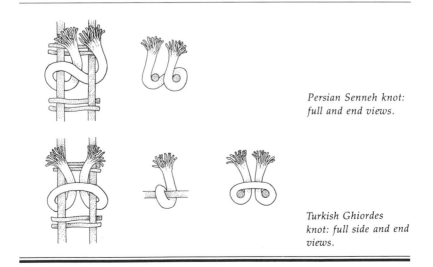

Persian Senneh knot: full and end views.

Turkish Ghiordes knot: full side and end views.

firmer weave, although the single strand of the Persian Senneh knot allows for more flowing outlines and apparently finer work simply because these knots occupy less space.

Despite their names, these two knots are used throughout the rug-weaving world. A very broad guideline to remember is that the farther east you go, the more frequently you will find the Senneh knot. Most of Turkey, western Persia and the Caucasus use the double Ghiordes knot, while central and eastern Persia, India and China prefer the single Senneh knot. However, you will come across many exceptions. To really know which knot has been used, bend a rug back on itself along its weft thread and look at the tufted ends of the pile. If the ends are together and the horizontal part of the thread is wrapped around the warp on both sides of the knot, it is a double Turkish Ghiordes knot. If you can see a warp thread separating the two tufted ends of the knot, it is a single Persian Senneh knot. You may need a magnifying glass to see the difference when the knot count is very high; and a drop or two of water will smooth the fibers and help make the knot stand out more clearly.

KELIM WEAVING

As I have previously described, kelim ends form the base of the fringe for most oriental rugs and their purpose is to prevent the knots from unraveling. However, kelim weaving is also used to create entire rugs. These pieces are woven flat, rather like tapestry. They have no pile and are almost perfectly reversible. Their designs will be angular and in most cases consist of simple geometric patterns. The colorings of kelims are similar to those of the pile rugs, though less elaborate. The method of weaving kelims is rather different from that of rugs. To form the pattern, a shuttle is used to carry the cotton or woolen thread across the warp—not from one side of the rug to the other but just as far as the pattern and color dictate. Then the thread is turned back on itself to go in the direction from which it came, finishing on the same side that it started. The design is thus formed by different colored threads that meet but do not join. If you hold a kelim woven in this way up to the light, you will see the gaps quite easily.

If for some reason the weaver wants to make a very dense kelim, then she will still use the same style of weaving but will link adjoining colors by passing the thread around a shared warp thread. However, the gaps which are found in most kelims are popular and can be used to emphasize parts of the design.

Kelims are usually woven from cotton but sometimes pure

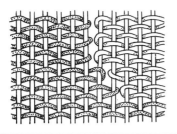

A section of kelim weaving.

wool kelims are made, too. Because a rug's pile is what protects the knots and kelims have no pile, they are unsuitable to use as floor coverings in areas where they will be constantly walked on. After only a few years of this sort of treatment, the cotton will be quite thin and eventually the rug will shred.

Kelims are designed to be used for tent hangings, curtains, divan coverings and decoration. Narrow strips of kelim weave are made to decorate the harnesses of camels and horses. And although the topsides of saddlebags are woven with a pile in exactly the same way as a rug, the underside of the entire saddlebag is typically woven as a simple kelim. However, the corners and outer edges of the underside of the saddlebag may be trimmed with pile to protect the animal from the rubbing of the harsher kelim surface. Often all four corners of saddlebags are decorated with colored tassels which swing back and forth and help keep away the flies. Any piece, such as saddlebags, grain sacks or pillow rugs, with tassels sewn onto each corner is not meant to be used on the floor. It may be part of the elaborate trappings made to decorate a rich man's horse or part of a nomad's portable "chest of drawers." The chest of drawers consists of a number of bags woven in various shapes and sizes in which the nomad keeps his clothes, matches, tobacco, shoes, food, combs, valuables and pots and pans. All these little bags can be conveniently hung up inside his tent.

The Indian version of a kelim is called a *dhurri*. Dhurris are also reversible and have angular designs or simple stripes, with an occasional figure worked in. They are made of cotton, which is easily laundered, and were originally designed to use in the hot steamy months of the year when pile rugs would have been unsuitable.

THE DELIBERATE MISTAKE

In any of the true Persian or Turkish rugs, it should be possible to discover the Deliberate Mistake. Many of the Moslem faith believe that only Allah makes things perfectly; therefore, to weave a perfectly designed rug would be to risk offending Him.

I once knew a repairer of rugs who held this belief so firmly that he was in constant trouble with his employer. He could (and his employer knew that he could) do such fine work that it was impossible to see the repair even under a magnifying glass. However, just before finishing work on each rug, he would make a deliberate mistake. This error, small as it was, meant that the repair could be detected. He explained that, although he was afraid of offending his employer, he was even more fearful of offending Allah. However, the repairer said his prayers very faithfully and was sure that Allah would see that he didn't lose his job. For years his boss tried to convince the repairer to do just one perfect repair. The pieces he worked on were so rare that they were almost always destined to hang in museums. But the repairer remained true to his belief. Allah would make it clear to the museums and they would understand—which, of course, they did.

The original Deliberate Mistake is usually made in the execution of the pattern, not in the preparation of the dyes or in the knotting of the rug. Genuine Deliberate Mistakes are very difficult to spot. I once studied a rug for ages before discovering

A nomad's "chest of drawers."

that, among hundreds of tiny flowers, one miniature petal was woven in a different color from all the rest.

SIGNATURE RUGS

The importance of a weaver's signature on a rug is, in my opinion, dubious. A masterpiece is a masterpiece whether or not it is signed. Many people disagree with me about the value of a signature so I shall simply say that I personally never worry as to whether or not a rug that I am thinking of buying is signed. In the trade, what matters is where the rug was made and how well it was made. The quality of the materials, the fineness of the knots, the beauty of the colors and designs—these things are far more valuable than a signature. The fact that some weavers sign their work of course means that they are proud of it; but many more weavers who are equally proud do not sign. They feel that the quality of their work speaks for them, and besides, the addition of a signature could spoil the symmetry of the design.

Most retailers disagree with my attitude towards signatures, so a signed rug usually does cost more in a retail store. A signature makes a good selling point and a flamboyant signature is often used as an excuse for raising the price—but, in my view, it doesn't raise the value.

REVERSIBLE RUGS

Reversible rugs, *doruye*, have completely different designs and colors on each side. They are made by tying rows of knots on alternate sides of the rug; thus, these pieces have pile on both sides.

Doruye are extremely rare. I have seen only two examples of them in my life. Unfortunately, I saw both at the very beginning of my career in rugs when I knew too little to appreciate them (I remember thinking that they were "quite nice novelties"). Both rugs were silk and each one had a warm side (pinks, golds, ivory) and a cool side (blues, greens, frosty white). I was told that the pink-gold side was for use in the winter and the blue-green side helped you to feel cool in the heat of the summer. Both rugs had central medallion designs on their warm sides while the reverse side of one rug had a garden design and the reverse side of the other had a design of a vase filled with flowers. Although both of these rugs were Persian (made either in Qum or Tabriz), reversible rugs are known to occur once in a while in Turkey and Armenia.

PLAIN RUGS

Completely plain rugs, woven in a single solid color, are quite common among modern Chinese rugs and, more especially, among the modern Indian pieces. Anyone who is interested in oriental rugs will have noticed these thick, woolly, white (sometimes pastel-colored) rugs that are in so many of the department stores today.

Totally plain rugs are unknown among the work of the Persian and Turkish weavers. For a Persian or Turkish weaver to produce such a rug would make no sense. It would be as though an artist were to regard his blank store-bought canvas as a finished painting. For the oriental artist-weavers, rugs are like windows through which they can view their history and their dreams. A plain rug would be like a window with the blinds drawn, through which nothing can be seen.

A nomadic Baluchi rug with vases of immortality arranged in an allover design.

CHAPTER THREE

Dyeing to Know

Color is part of the essence of an oriental rug. It is as important in a rug as it is in a painting; the beauty of the rug depends on it. Imaginative, artistic coloring can mean that a poorly woven rug is nevertheless delightful. If the colors are "wrong," even the most technically perfect piece "misses." The colors may shine as they do in a stained-glass window; they may be rich and dark or clear pastels or even, as in the case of the Fars rugs (made near the Persian town of Shiraz), contrasting tones of undyed wools. What matters is that the color statement should add a dimension of beauty and be so subtle that you will never tire of looking at it. The glowing wine reds of Afghanistan, the pure blues of the antique Chinese rugs, the soft brick reds of Asia Minor all have this quality. Each region, town and tribe tends to remain true to its own particular color theme, even in these mobile days. The designs of the rugs change far more easily than their basic colors.

In the cool climates of the north we enjoy the sunshine—we even bathe in it. The harsh sun of the tropical plains and in particular of the deserts is another matter. For the people who live in the hot arid regions, the constant glare of the sun is exhausting. This is one of the reasons why many oriental rugs are made in strong dark colors. Strong, because all color appears weaker in very bright light; and dark to give relief to sun-dazzled eyes. Pale, softly colored rugs are woven but only in the cooler parts of the rug-producing countries. So that any rug you select

Many nomadic tents are made of dark-colored cloth, which is restful to sun-dazzled eyes.

will last, it is important (if you want a rug with gentle colors) that you choose one that was woven that way, not bleached afterwards.

VEGETABLE DYES

Originally, all dyes were made exclusively from animal and vegetable substances. The freely growing wild madder root is used to make various warm *reds*. The older the plant, the deeper the shade of red. The roots of plants which are over eight years old produce a purplish wine red. Different types of crushed cochineal insects make either a bright magenta color or a brilliant crimson when they are boiled in the dye vat. To make the vivid "Turkey red" the madder is mixed with milk which has been fermented for exactly thirty days. Ox blood is sometimes used to make brownish reds.

All the vegetable-dye *blues* are made from the indigo plant, which grows well in the warm countries of the East. The depth of blue depends on how often the wool is dipped into the dye to which sugary fixatives such as honey or dates have been added. This is done to overcome the fact that indigo is not soluble in water. If you rub wool dyed with indigo plants, it will often leave a blue mark on your hand.

The *yellow* dyes are made from the saffron crocus, vine leaves or milkwort (Isperek), as well as other plants such as reseda and buckthorn (although overbright if used in large areas, buckthorn is a very fast dye). Pomegranate skin makes a rather muddy yellow, but when it is blended with metal salts it can become olive or lime green. Other *greens* are made from turmeric berries and vine leaves. A mix of blue and yellow can also produce various greens, just as blue and red can be combined to make *purple*, but these kinds of combinations are frequently unstable.

Orange colors are made from henna or vine leaves. Persian berries, madder and pomegranate skins can produce a golden *brown*. Other browns are made from catechu (or cutch), walnut shells and oak bark. *Blackish* colors are made either by mixing henna with indigo or else by using logwood (brazilwood) combined with ferrous sulfate. Sadly, this iron salt is corrosive; in time it eats away the wool down to the warp threads, which is why many old rugs have an embossed look.

The natural blacks, greys and browns of the wool are, of course, also used, but like all undyed animal fibers, they tend to fade. *White* is simply the natural color of the wool. The Turkoman nomads often give it an ivory cast by curing it in the smoke from their fires.

ANILINE DYES

For many hundreds of years vegetable dyes were the only ones available to the weavers. However, in 1856 when Sir William Henry Perkin (1838–1907) was just eighteen years old, he dis-

Most dye stuffs are ground and sifted as a first step in preparing the dyes.

Here a camel does the work of grinding dye stuffs.

covered the aniline dye. Aniline as a substance had been around since 1823 and Sir William, who attended the Royal College of Chemistry in England, had been busy trying to produce a synthetic quinine when he discovered the aniline dye. The first aniline-dye color was violet. Realizing the importance of his discovery, Sir William and his father soon set up a factory to make the dye commercially. In the following years many other bright, attractive colors were developed.

Because aniline dyes were both inexpensive and easy to use, huge amounts were imported into Turkey and Persia in the late 1860s. They became increasingly popular and by 1890 were being used in all the rug-producing areas. Unfortunately, aniline dyes are unsound: reds fade to mauve, blues turn to brownish greys, and yellows become greenish browns. These changes began to take place in aniline-dyed rugs almost as soon as the rugs were off the looms; the reputation (and the export trade) of oriental rugs was being seriously damaged. In 1903 aniline was outlawed by Persia. Horrifying penalties were imposed: if a dye house was suspected of using aniline, it could be burned to the ground; if a weaver was caught using aniline-dyed wool, his right hand could be cut off. Understandably, the use of aniline dyes in Persia ceased, although the surrounding countries continued to use them.

CHROMATIC DYES

In the 1920s and 1930s the European chemists developed new synthetic dyes. These turned out to be more permanent than many of the original vegetable dyes and equally beautiful. The most successful of the modern dyes are made in Germany. The use of "chromatic" dyes throughout the rug-producing countries may not have actually added to the beauty of the weaver's palette, but they have expanded its range. Most oriental rugs are now made using a combination of chromatic and vegetable dyes. This in no way devalues them. The problem lies *only* with the anilines. I am constantly amazed that many otherwise well-informed writers continue to mislead people into believing that modern synthetic dyes are unsubtle and unsound. It is true that they were, but that was over sixty years ago. These new chromatics are permanent, and beautiful rugs are made with them.

A few years ago in the Turkish village of Hereke, I was introduced to the white-mustachioed senior dye master who presided over the workshop where the finest of the silk Hereke rugs are woven. The light, airy room was large and filled with rows of little girls who giggled shyly as I walked about their looms, looking at the marvelous rugs they were making. Turkish popular music blared from the transistor radios. It was so loud that conversation was impossible. In a corner at the far end of the room was the silk-store, where all the silk was kept. Retreating from the noise of the radios, I went in. It was like entering a treasure vault filled with precious gems. The skeins of silks flashed so brilliantly in the dimmer light of the storehouse that their jewel colors dazzled me. Emerald, ruby, silver, gold and sapphire shone beside aquamarine, jade and coral. Carrying some of the silk outside so that I could see the colors more clearly, I remarked to the elderly dye master how incredibly lovely they were. Good dye masters are very proud of their skill, the secrets of which they carefully guard. The coral and jade silks were especially beautiful. I risked saying how impossible it would be to achieve such subtle colors using chromatic dyes. He hooted with laughter and led me back to the silk-store where he pointed out the open cans of synthetic dyes that were his "secret" formula. Unlike vegetable dyes, chromatics can be blended to create an infinite range of colors and still remain perfectly sound. Of course, some of the dyes he used were vegetable ones but an equal number came from the various cans lying around on the floor, clearly labeled with the manufacturer's name and address in Germany.

However, because of "expert-sponsored" prejudice, most merchants will tell you their rugs are vegetable-dyed. In fact, they are probably made with a mixture of vegetable-dyed material and chromatic-dyed material. I have also watched many dye masters preparing dyes and seen them adding a hefty pinch or two of chromatic dyes to the vegetable ones. To make them "clear" or give them "strong life" is the usual explanation given. In terms of the price of a rug, the possible beauty of its coloring, as well as the skill needed to create the subtlety of shade present in hand-dyed wool, there is no difference. New rugs made with pure vegetable dyes (and there are a few) and rugs made using a combination of dyes are of equal value. The cases where the chromatic dyes are undesirable are when the wools have been clumsily hand-dyed in crude, harsh colors. These cheap, coarsely knotted "bazaar rugs" are made only for commercial reasons. And if the wools have been industrially machine-spun and then machine-dyed, the process destroys a lot of the wool's natural lanolin.

To know if wool has been dyed by hand or by machine, look very closely at the face of the rug. Hand-dyed wools, the color of which even from a foot or two away may appear completely uniform, will under close examination turn out to be irregular. The irregularities may be minute, especially if the colors you are looking at are dyed in chromatic indigo or madder, but they will be there. Machine-dyed wools, on the other hand, will look completely uniform. There are no variations to give depth to their coloring. Rugs made from machine-dyed wool quickly become boring—the antithesis of what an oriental rug is all about.

THE PROCESS OF DYEING

Most dye masters are independent artisans. They work to order and sometimes also sell their colored wools in the bazaar. The main artery of the huge Covered Bazaar at Isfahan in Persia is Gheisarieh. Its high arched ceiling is intersected at intervals with wide holes to allow some ventilation and shadowy light to illuminate the crowded narrow pathway below. Lining both sides of the pathway are the small, open-faced stores that sell everything. Here you may buy live chickens or bolts of cloth, chunks of turquoise, vegetables, medicines, records, rice, golden jewelry or pungent spices. Rugs, plastic combs and the feet of butchered donkeys are also sold. The deafening noise of copper being beaten to make pots and pans is only topped by strident voices bargaining as though their lives depended on the outcome.

If you were to follow one of the side turnings at the far corner of the bazaar, close to where the big bundles of fluffy undyed

Wool stored in a side room of the dye master's cavern.

wool are sold, you would come to an ancient doorway. Beyond this is a dye master's cavern. The main part of the cavern is where the actual dyeing process takes place, with side rooms for storing the wool. The skeins of wool are first hand-spun and consequently the strands are irregular in their thickness. Then they are prepared with various mordants. According to the chosen color, the mordant might include, for example, common potash alum, egg white or tartaric acid. Soaking the wool in these mixtures enables the fibers of the material and the dye to unite. The wool is then plunged into one of several large caldrons in which the dyes are simmering. These huge earthenware or copper vats are heated by fires built at the base of each vat. This is to maintain the dyes at the appropriate temperatures while the wool is steeping for varying amounts of time. Because of the irregular thickness of the wool and the fats it contains, air bubbles often form on its surface, producing an uneven effect.

While the dye master is at work, carefully following ancient recipes which are so secret that they are passed only from father to son, no one other than his successor may speak to him. Usually few of the chemical processes of the recipes are understood by the dye masters, who intuitively create the wonderful colors. At

The dye master's assistant stirring the wool into the boiling dye.

The wool must steep at the right temperature for exactly the right amount of time if the color is to be perfect.

Judging the correct depth of color is an exacting art.

periodic intervals the dye master will remove batches of wool from the caldrons and hang them outside in the sun to set the dye. Most wool is immersed several times until a proper depth of color is achieved. Finally the wool is thoroughly rinsed in fresh water to remove the excess dye.

If you stand in the half-light of this Isfahan dye master's cavern, crowded with its steaming caldrons, and look out through the arch, you see his yard. Filled with brilliant wools drying in the sun, it is a breathtaking sight.

TESTING THE SOUNDNESS OF DYES

Knowing whether or not the material of any rug you are considering buying has been correctly dyed is important. If shortcuts were taken so that the dyes are unsound, two problems in particular occur. The first is that the rug will be difficult to clean. If you spill any liquid on it, even a glass of plain water, the rug might be spoiled. When poor-quality or wrongly blended dyes (vegetable or synthetic) are used or when the dyes are not properly fixed, if the colors become wet they may bleed into each other. The outlines of the pattern are then blurred and the rug looks messy. Serious "color run" drops a rug's "value points" way down (see Chapter 9 for a description of value points). The second possible problem, although less immediate, could be equally serious. Unsound dyes mean that any rug could drastically change or even lose its color. For example, if you bought a rug because you loved its clear coloring and a few months later the colors had all turned greyish-brown, you would probably be disappointed.

The Handkerchief Test

Of course, no honest, reliable dealer would knowingly sell you a rug with unsound colors. However, there is a simple test that you can do for yourself. Spit on a clean white handkerchief (saliva is alkaline) and, rubbing briskly, test each of the colors in turn. Check as you do so to see if any of the dyes stain the handkerchief. So long as the cloth remains color-free, you have no problem. If it stains, the extent of the problem depends on the extent of the stain. Some vegetable dyes will always slightly stain the handkerchief. The operative word here is *slightly*. In these cases, slight staining is neither considered a fault nor

The dye master in his yard.

should it cause you major problems—unless you plan to take your rug swimming, as one of my clients actually did, in a heavily chlorinated pool. He had heard that chlorine was used to give rugs a shiny look, so after adding a great deal of extra chlorine, he dunked the rug. It is true that a two percent chlorine wash would have done little harm, but he administered a far greater dose. Deep staining of your handkerchief, however, is very bad news. It means either that the dye was substandard or that the fixative failed. Never buy a new rug that completely fails the handkerchief test. If you already own one, I suggest you auction it.

As always, there is an exception. I might possibly advise you to buy (but more likely, to keep) a rug with loose colors if it was made by nomads. They frequently dye their wool themselves and may not rinse it thoroughly enough. Consequently, a lot of loose dye remains. The excess dye can be removed by *professional* oriental rug cleaners so that little if any of the color runs. An old rug, forty years old or more, that fails the handkerchief test is likely to have been "painted." In this case, it is unlikely that the colors will drastically change, although they will probably fade and also bleed if they get wet. Old painted pieces are not too difficult to recognize—they have a kind of dense, flat, lackluster look.

CHEMICAL BLEACHING

The presence of lanolin in the wool of an oriental rug which has been walked on for ten to twenty years (ideally by stockinged feet) and has generally been treated kindly enables it to develop a natural gloss or patina. You might almost believe that top-quality wool had been turned into silk. Also, the effects of time will eventually mellow the colors in every rug. Many antique pieces owe much of their beauty to the weird, exquisite ways in which their colors have "settled." But the Western world really does not like to wait. (Television shows such as "Mission Impossible" have taught us that any problem can be solved in sixty minutes.) So, because the Western markets demanded "instant antiquing," the chemical wash was developed in London.

Each year, before they are re-exported, hundreds of rugs are bathed in various chemical solutions which bleach their bright colors to the more popular pastels. Other chemicals are then used to give the wool an instant patina, but these are relatively harmless and may even enhance poor-quality wool. However, even the most up-to-date *strong* chemical bleaching takes years off the life span of a rug. In some cases, the situation is acute: Afghanistan produces rugs that are woven in yellow gold which have become so fashionable these days that demand has outstripped supply. Consequently, many rugs that were originally red are chemically bleached when they arrive in the West. Unfortunately, the wool of these bleached rugs tends to become brittle and break after a short time.

To tell whether a rug has been woven in natural gold or bleached, break open the pile and look at the base of the rug where the knot is tied. If you see a pinkish color, you may be sure that the rug was bleached and it would be advisable not to buy it. "G.W. Afghan" on a tag should mean "golden-woven"; in fact, it has now come to mean "golden-washed" in most retail stores. When I recently asked a salesman whether a rug was golden-woven or golden-washed, he told me with great authority that both terms meant the same thing.

In other types of rugs, look at the back if you suspect that it has been washed in a strong chemical bleach. If it has, there will be little difference of shade; the back will look almost as pale as the front. If the back is bright, it means either that the rug is genuinely softly colored or that it has been deliberately "sun-bleached" in Persia (a natural way of softening colors by leaving rugs out in the sun). Or the rug may have undergone a light, comparatively harmless chemical wash which will reduce its useful life expectancy by only ten percent or so.

THE USE OF COLORS

It really is more sensible to choose your rug from among the unbleached variety. Regardless of what you may be told, rugs are *woven* in marvelous colors, many combinations of which are gentle and easy to live with. Another good reason to avoid buying a chemically bleached rug is that the bleaching destroys the balance and the depth of the colors. Rugs generally appear much paler than the actual colors of the fibers from which they are made. You may think you are looking at a pale rug; or perhaps it's a white one. Nevertheless, unless it has been bleached, the white parts will actually be grey, cream or ivory. Try placing a sheet of white paper on top of the rug. Better still, sneak out one of the knots from the back with a pin and put this tuft of wool in the center of the paper. Then look at it with half-closed eyes. You'll be surprised just how dark all the individual colors in a "pale" rug really are. It is precisely this depth of color that allows the different colors of the rug to blend. Yet the effect of the balance and blend of the colors, is, indeed, soft and pale.

The number of colors used in any single oriental rug is difficult to judge. A rug may seem to blaze with dozens of different colors. Count them—two to fifteen is the general range and few rugs have more than nine colors. Bright colors are prevented from clashing with one another by being outlined in cream, black, beige or grey. Although these thin lines may be invisible from even a short distance away, they do in fact help to create a harmony of coloring by smoothing out the tonal balance.

ARBRUSHES

When you see a stripe of a different tone (occasionally it may be a different color) running horizontally right across the face of a rug, it is described as an *arbrush* (some American dealers say "hairbrush"). Arbrushes happen for a number of reasons. They may be woven deliberately in a different shade of wool to cheer up a plain, open-field background which the weaver felt was monotonous. Or they may be there to please those buyers (often Iranian ones) who will never buy a rug unless it *is* arbrushed. In both these cases, the arbrush is designed as a series of thin, delicate stripes closely paralleling each other to form the main stripe, usually an inch or more wide.

Accidental arbrushes happen when the weaver runs out of wool and has to finish the rug with wool dyed in a different batch. (Have you ever been knitting a sweater, run out of wool and had to buy a fresh supply? Finding a precisely matching shade can be a problem even in the United States where wools are machine-dyed.) Arbrushes also appear when a rug is "washed," even if no bleach is involved and the wash is a light one, given just to add luster to the wool. However, if after this treatment, the rug remains arbrush-free, you can be almost certain that one won't turn up later on. In chemical-free rugs, arbrushes may take years to evolve. The effects of light and air slowly cause changes in the chemistry of the mordants and the dyes. Many antique rugs develop wonderful arbrushes over the decades.

Some people simply don't like arbrushes and, in fact, some arbrushes are unattractive. So if you would prefer a rug without one, there are plenty around. Only please don't insist on a rug with entirely uniform coloring. Their variegated colors are almost certainly part of what attracted you to oriental rugs in the first place.

THE SYMBOLISM OF COLORS

According to where a rug is made, each of its colors may have a slightly different meaning, although the general idea will be the same. Besides understanding these meanings, you will also need to interpolate between the colors. Green, for instance, is a self-assertive color and blue is a tranquil one; so a greeny blue can mean firmness. Whether it does or not will depend on the other colors in the rug.

White is the most "open" of all the colors. It represents peace, purity and, being the color most easily stained, grief. In the Orient white is the color of mourning.

Blue means tranquil peace. It is the color of heaven, eternity and the night sky. It is a quiet color and is often used to symbolize thoughtfulness and meditation, high ideals, oneness, and spiritual, devoted joy. In China, dark blue means relaxed but powerful strength or authority. It also means solitude. Blue of any shade represents water as it reflects the sky. Other meanings are sensitivity, loyalty and contentment.

Red is the most vibrantly alive of all the colors. It means great joy, happiness and success. It is a powerful, energetic color

*An unusually quiet
moment in the bazaar.*

and represents leadership and government. Red also represents growth, creativity and battles, as well as vitality, passion and desire. Red is always actively outgoing and symbolizes the fullness of life.

Yellow, the color of the sun, is used to represent plentiful riches, glory and active power. It also means a release from burdens and the attainment of hoped-for happiness. In China, yellow is only used for rugs with a royal connection. The Chinese emperors often wore gold or yellow and regarded these colors as their personal property. It was a very unwise weaver indeed who wove a rug in yellow and failed to present it to the ruler.

Green means constancy, the spring which always returns. Paradise is green with plants and flowering trees. Green is also a proud, self-assertive color. It means recognition, superior attainment and an active desire to lead others to a more useful life. Green is said to have been the color of Mohammed's coat and so is regarded by those of the Moslem religion as being the holy color. It is a color the weavers use sparingly and with great respect.

Brown is the color of acceptance, the fruitful earth (harvest) and fertility; it also means roots. In nomadic rugs brown is frequently used to express a need for their own earth or home, a place where they may comfortably rest. (The little houses they sometimes picture in their rugs are another expression of this usually unobtainable dream; they are always searching for new grass with which to feed their flocks.)

Orange means devotion, tenderness, a sympathy and high regard for others. Orange is often used as a background color for the marriage-tree design rugs as it means human love.

Purple is a very self-important color and is often used to represent the ruler, sometimes of the country (excepting China) and sometimes of the household. It expresses the determination to make dreams come true and so is the color of magic spells and self-identity.

Mauve means a wish to be admired and made the center of everyone else's world. It also shows a concern for self-preservation and is a watered-down version of purple's meanings.

Grey is the color of secrets. It means seclusion and noninvolvement, withdrawn separation and neutrality.

Black means both destruction and the unknown. It means silent nothingness. It also means a peaceful end.

Girls from a village in the Bakhtiari region weaving a carpet with a Persian-garden design.

CHAPTER FOUR

Elephants and Gardens

The world of oriental rugs is peopled by thousands of skilled, talented artists who, as I've mentioned in Chapter 2, more often than not don't bother to sign their names to the masterpieces they may take years to create. One of the first things to learn about rugs is how to "read" them to know where they were made.

The name of any particular rug indicates the town, village or tribe from which it came. If, for instance, a rug were made in the town of Tabriz, it would be called a Persian Tabriz. Rugs do not take their names from the birthplace of the weaver, but only from the place in which the rugs were made. For instance, if a girl from a Turkoman tribe married into a Baluchi tribe, the rugs she wove would be called Baluchi. Although she would probably continue to use the designs from the Turkoman tribe, the colors and materials would be those typical of the Baluchis. Purists may disagree with this method of classifying rugs, but it is a simple and practical way of differentiating among rugs and one that is understood worldwide.

I want to give you a useful, overall understanding of rugs. Later, if one particular type of rug sparks your interest, you can fully investigate its individual area. (If I had been told at the beginning of my career that, for instance, each rug from the Caucasus must be exactly named, the prospect would have been rather daunting.)

One of the fascinating aspects of "reading" rugs is discovering the meanings behind their designs. Almost all of the basic designs are over four centuries old and many of them were already ancient in the days of Moses. The history of a people was recorded in the rugs they wove: battles won and lost, important leaders, religion, superstitions and tragic love stories (the Persians are especially fond of these).

There are more than twenty rug-producing areas in the world, but for the sake of simplicity I shall divide them into six major groups: Persia, Turkey, Russia, India, China and North Africa. Persia is now Iran, of course, but I will refer to Persia throughout the book because the rugs are known by that name. In general, Turkish is used to describe rugs from Turkey and the region around it. When a dealer is selling a Turkish rug, especially if it is an old or antique piece, he may refer to it as being Anatolian (the ancient name for Asia Minor), particularly if he doesn't know the exact origin of the rug. Russia will include Bulgaria, Romania and the famous Caucasus region as well as the Turkoman region which borders Afghanistan, Persia and the Caspian Sea. I shall include Afghanistan in the Russian Turkoman group, although this is geographically inaccurate. India will include Pakistan. North Africa will include Morocco, Libya and Egypt.

THE MEANING OF DESIGNS

Persia produces over four thousand different types of rugs. In general, you may expect a rug to have been made in Persia if it has a relatively elaborate design, either curvilinear or rectilinear, showing flowers, animals and birds in a wide variety of colors. The range of tonal effect of Persian rugs is, broadly speaking, medium to light. Red is a popular color, used in every shade from cherry through scarlet to soft coral. Blues are also widely used, especially the very deep indigo blue that appears so often as the background color.

Persian rugs are generally well constructed. They may be made of wool pile on a cotton warp, wool with silk on a cotton warp, or wool on a silk warp. There are also pure silk rugs and pure wool nomadic rugs.

Perhaps the best-known Persian design is that of the *prayer arch,* which is used in all prayer rugs. In its simplest form (often made by nomads) this is a rectangular design woven parallel to the edges of the rug. The most common version is where one end of the rectangle has its corners angled off to form a pointed

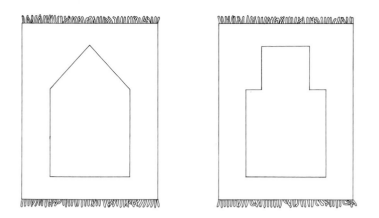

Pointed and rectangular prayer arches, or mihrabs.

arch, a *mihrab*. When a Moslem kneels to pray, he rests his forehead within the mihrab, which represents the doorway of the revered Sacred Mosque in Mecca. If the rug is made by nomads, the mihrab is sometimes further simplified so that two-thirds of the way up, the rectangle is narrowed abruptly to form a small square at one end of the rug.

Usually prayer rugs will have only a single mihrab except when the rug is intended to be used by the family simultaneously or is intended for the mosque. Rugs with multiple mihrabs are produced occasionally in Persia (and in the Caucasus region of Russia), but they are more typical of Turkish rugs. (It is customary for people to donate a rug to their mosque; then when someone goes to the mosque and prays on the rug, that person will often say a prayer for the donor of the rug. The more rugs a person donates, the more prayers will be said for him.)

Prayer rugs made by nomadic tribes or in small Persian

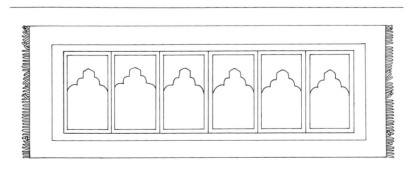

Turkish Saph design, showing multiple prayer arches.

Many rugs besides prayer rugs depict the tree of life. In this Isfahan the tree itself is the main design, set within a flowering forest.

villages often have centers which are either plain and undecorated or are filled with small stylized flowers, stars or a stylized tree of life, symbolic of the garden of paradise. This tree of life is represented by a straight line drawn up the center of the rug, which represents the trunk of the tree; short horizontal lines drawn across the trunk represent the branches. In town and workshop rugs, this garden is often highly elaborate. Streams flow, small trees blossom, and animals and birds abound. If the design is curvilinear and the prayer arch is decorated with lifelike flowers, vases, trees or garden scenes, the rug is probably from a Persian workshop (but it could be a copy of a Persian design made in India or Pakistan, in which case it will have a very high gloss to the wool and a bright white cotton fringe).

The *tree of life* represents eternal life. This design occurs mainly in Persia, especially in the towns of Isfahan, Qum and Tabriz where they produce remarkably lifelike trees. The trees grow from the base of the rug, starting just within its borders and continuing to fill the entire field. The leafy branches are spread and dotted with flowers and birds. Often there will be a stream or pool at the foot of the tree and perhaps a few small animals.

Occasionally you may find a rug where two trees of life, their branches entwined, are growing within the same rug. These are called *marriage-tree* rugs, most often found among the work of the weavers of Tabriz and Qum. They symbolize a forthcoming marriage (you may notice among the branches that small birds' nests have been added—with obvious significance). Sometimes a main branch of one of the trees will appear to have been sawn off; this means that it is a second marriage for one of the partners.

The *vase of immortality* is a "one-way" design in which the vase is shaped rather like a Greek urn which may or may not have handles. The vase is at the foot of the rug beneath an archway and is filled with flowers, usually roses, with the tallest flower in the center reaching up towards the top of the arch—a variation of the tree-of-life design. Roses and other flowers decorate the background of the rug.

While small trees are widely used throughout Persia, the *weeping-willow* design stands for sorrow and death. The *evergreen cypress* means eternal life. A rug with four small cypress trees in each corner means that it was made to cover a coffin. It is an oriental tradition to use branches of the cypress to indicate a home that is in mourning and cypress twigs are often placed within the coffin of the dead to provide strength for the journey to the next world.

The *garden-of-paradise* design can be either a one-way pattern or have a medallion at the center with a flower-filled forest around it. It is often depicted as being alive with animals and birds as well as flowers and flowering trees (see page 114).

The classical *Persian-garden* design, to which I referred in Chapter 1, is nowadays usually represented as a series of four- to six-inch (10 to 15 cm.) squares which form a grid covering the central field of the rug. Within each of the squares is a different picture showing the various aspects of a garden. Some squares may contain small trees or flowers, while others show deer,

A Kashan rug with a prayer arch, a vase of immortality, and a hanging lamp included in the design.

lambs or birds. Occasionally you may notice a square that contains a simple drawing of the house to which the garden belongs. The lines of the grid itself represent the water channels which irrigate the garden. The border framing the Persian-garden design rugs is usually uncomplicated and there are usually not more than five borders to a rug. (See page 66.)

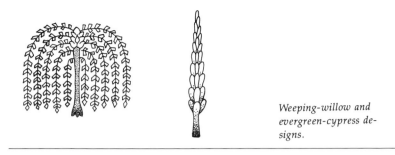

Weeping-willow and evergreen-cypress designs.

A second, quite rare interpretation of this design is the *archaeological garden*, sometimes found among the weaving of the people of the Persian holy city of Qum. In these rugs, the scenes of flowers and trees are replaced by drawings of urns, jugs and various pots. Sometimes these are decorated with faces, either on the pots themselves or on their handles. Aside from the theory that these drawings are based on finds from excavation sites, little is known about the symbolism of the archaeological-garden rugs of Qum.

Versions of the central *medallion* design are used throughout most of the rug-weaving world, with the exceptions of Turkmenistan and Afghanistan. The center point of the medallion represents the eye of an all-seeing deity. It is believed that the design is based on the lotus flower which has always been regarded as sacred, growing as it does with its roots in rank mud and its blossom turned to heaven. The medallion design is usually chosen for rugs that are intended to decorate a mosque, in which a complementary medallion design is frequently part of the architecture, that is, the ceiling of the mosque. The *teardrop medallion* (see pages 78–79), typical of the town of Kashan, symbolizes God's tears (the tears being the two points at either end of a slightly elongated sphere).

Medallion design.

The *allover* design is not, strictly speaking, a design. Rather, it is the name used to describe any pattern (apart from the repeating squares of the Persian-garden design) that has no focal point as, for example, a medallion, vase or prayer-arch design would provide. An allover pattern is one where the same motif is repeated in rows throughout the rug, limited only by the design of the borders.

A small round rosette surrounded by feather-shaped leaves and arranged in an allover pattern is called the *Herati* design. It is a motif widely used in Persia as well as in India, but the Herati pattern probably originated in the town of Herat in west-northwest Afghanistan. It is thought to symbolize the small fishes that, at the time of the full moon, come up to just beneath the surface of the water to swim in the moon's reflection. Thus, the Herati design is sometimes referred to as the *fish* design.

The familiar paisley design (often used in the West as a pattern for men's ties) originated in Persia where it is called *boteh*. It may have come to Persia via ancient Egypt as an ear of wheat, representing immortality, but this is not certain. Boteh means "leaf motif," usually the palmetto leaf. Because of their shape and texture, these leaves were often dried and used by the Persians as paper on which prayers could be written. So, naturally, the form of the boteh was incorporated into their rugs, particularly prayer rugs. Botehs are commonly used across the base of the prayer arch together with flowers as part of the symbol for the garden of paradise. Botehs may also be pictured in squares of the Persian-garden design, where they are meant to represent a view of palm trees.

Botehs are woven in a variety of sizes, large ones being six by three and a half inches (15 × 9 cm.), down to *boteh-miri*, which are usually no taller than two to two and a half inches (5 to 6.5 cm.). The boteh motif may appear as individual leaves placed, for example, in each corner of a rug or it may be used in a chain formation throughout an entire border; sometimes botehs outline a central medallion. Quite often they appear in an allover

Herati (fish) design.

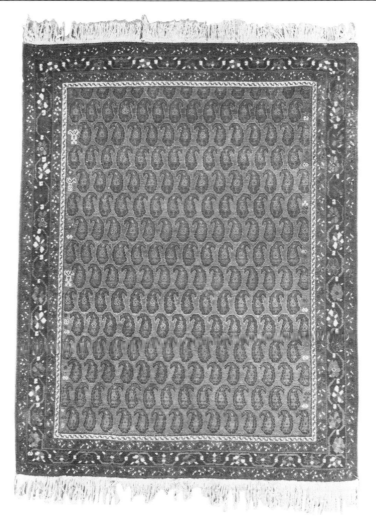

An Afshar rug, unusual for its allover boteh design.

design, where row after row of botehs fill the entire field of the rug. In the green highland area of Seraband, in the west-southwest of Persia, weavers seldom use any other pattern, so that the name Seraband has come to be used not only for pieces produced in this region but also to describe the allover boteh design.

The crests of the botehs usually face in alternating directions from row to row. One of the loveliest pieces I ever saw had an allover boteh design. It had been woven in Qum with a fine knot count of over 400 per square inch, so that the botehs had a delicate lacy quality. The background color was soft terra-cotta

A Qum rug with a hunting design.

and the botehs were woven in delphinium blue, ivory and mossy green. The rows of botehs dancing across the surface of the rug looked like small waves rippling across the sea. (Sadly, as so often happens when you're in the trade, I had to sell the rug to a young American client who took it with her to the Philippines. At least I know it went to a good home; she had saved her money for more than two years just to buy the rug.)

Besides the theory that the origins of the boteh are purely botanical, there are two other rather more romantic theories. One is that the boteh represents a flame, a design conceived by the Parsees who worshipped fire. The other theory is that the boteh commemorates the capitulation of one of Persia's early rulers who, having lost a battle, was forced to sign a document surrendering his throne and royal status. The story is that he was so embittered by the defeat that, when the moment came for him to sign, he drew his dagger and made a deep cut in his wrist. Then, after dipping the edge of his other fist in the blood, he made his mark on the document. After that, the sign of the fallen ruler's blood-stamp began to appear in rugs woven throughout the region.

Two other designs that are used often in Persian rugs are the *four seasons* and the *hunting* design. The four-seasons design divides the rug into four sections. In each quarter is a scene representing one of the four seasons of the year. These scenes are usually pastoral and drawn realistically. The origins of the four-seasons design are uncertain.

The hunting design, frequently found among the Persian Qum and Isfahan rugs, is thought to have originated at the court of a Turkish sultan in the early sixteenth century. The fierce Ottoman Turks had just conquered the region, and in the unusually peaceful times that followed, the sultan gathered together Chinese painters, poets and musicians, as well as expert carpet weavers. The hunting design shows huntsmen riding horses and spearing various unfortunate animals; they are accompanied by tame leopards (sometimes used to symbolize hounds).

PERSIA

The town of Kashan has produced some of Persia's finest classical rugs. (It also has the reputation of having supplied most of her assassins!) These rugs are well made of wool on a cotton warp and the traditional color used for the backgrounds of most rugs is either cherry red or dark blue. The designs of the classic Kashans are mainly the tear-drop medallion and the vase of immortality. The medallion design may have elaborate borders with a scattering of lotus flowers or roses over the central field, or elaborate borders with corner pieces on a plain field. The vase of immortality is placed at the center point of the base of the prayer arch, decorated with flowers and occasionally a small bird.

A Kashan rug with a tear-drop medallion on a plain field.

Since the 1920s, the weavers of Kashan have been producing pieces made specifically for the Western market. These rugs have ivory-colored backgrounds with designs woven in several shades of blue. The designs of these "white" Kashans, as they are known—even when pale blue or green is substituted for ivory—are abstract arabesques entwined around lotus-flower heads, with an inconspicuous medallion.

Rugs from the holy city of Qum may be made from either wool and silk or wool inlaid with silk. Their designs are usually curvilinear, showing flowers, birds and small animals. The formal prayer-arch pattern, incorporating the two *pillars of wisdom,* is often used, as well as the hunting design mentioned earlier.

There are two major clues to help you identify rugs from Qum. Firstly, almost without exception, somewhere within Qum

A Kashan rug with a tear-drop medallion on a field filled with flowers.

rugs you will find either touches or entire backgrounds of a soft turquoise–sky blue color (see color plate 1). This is the color of many of the rooftops in the holy city, and this exact blue does not seem to appear in rugs from any other area. Secondly, almost all of these pieces will have one fringe that is much shorter than the other. This is traditional in Qum and in many cases the short fringe will be left in the form of a kelim end.

Modern rugs made in the town of Kirman have a central, softly curving floral medallion. This medallion pattern is repeated in quarters, with one quarter placed in each of the four corners of the rug. The border designs are made up of flowers and scrolls and the field is open (woven in a single solid color). In general,

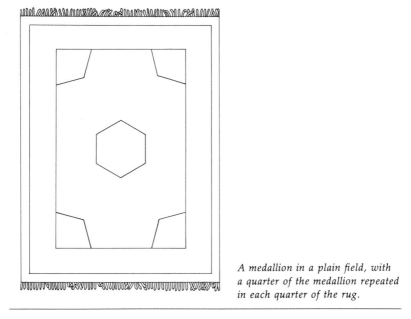

A medallion in a plain field, with a quarter of the medallion repeated in each quarter of the rug.

both modern and old Kirman pieces are made of wool on a cotton warp, with a pile of approximately half an inch (1.5 cm.). The old and antique Kirman rugs, the best of which are known as Kirman Laver, were more finely woven, the designs more complicated (rarely do they have an open field), the colors more varied (a medium geranium pink is typical). Usually these rugs will be only half the thickness of the modern pieces.

"Isfahan is half the world" or so the old Persian saying would have us believe. Once the capital city of Persia under the Saffavid Dynasty, it is very beautiful. Its graceful buildings are made of stone, the soft golden color of which is often echoed in their rugs. The azure and sapphire blue domes of its many mosques tower over the city, colors also echoed in the rugs woven there. Isfahan is dotted with picturesque gardens and flowering trees. The famous Covered Bazaar is there, built around the great square where centuries ago nobles played polo. The northwest of the city is bounded by a wide river over which is an arching bridge where the traffic of donkeys, goats and sheep mingles with Mercedes.

The best of the modern-day Isfahans are made from kurk (lamb's wool). They are woven on a silk warp and weft, unlike those pieces produced prior to 1910 when cotton was more usual; consequently the early rugs were also less closely woven than the best Isfahans made today. Today Isfahans are among the most

A Kirman rug with a medallion on an oval-shaped plain field and a typically elaborate border design.

finely knotted rugs in the world—500 knots to the square inch is quite normal. This means that their abstract designs are wonderfully well defined. Typical of Isfahan are graceful flowers and jewel-like medallions with lotus blossoms and curving leaves, all entwined with flowing tendrils and curving arabesques. These abstract designs, the outlines of which are often feathered, bring to mind the elaborately decorated ceilings of the mosques. The purest blues of every shade are used, blended with ivory (see color plate 2). Often a glowing deep red will be added or a bright gold or golden chestnut. The individual colors

The King's Mosque at Isfahan in winter.

in these rugs are among the richest in Persia. Occasionally, small birds may be included in a design, but this is more characteristic of the neighboring village of Nain.

The tiny village of Nain, where the houses are built of baked sand, also produces incredibly fine rugs, 450 knots per square inch being average. Many Iranian buyers consider Nain rugs equal to the work of Isfahan weavers. Nains are usually made of fine wool with the designs often outlined in silk. The major difference between Isfahan and Nain rugs is that the warp and weft threads of the Nains are made from fine cotton.

Nain produces abstract designs similar to those of Isfahan, but in general Nains are more likely to be representational designs of flowers, butterflys or small birds. Usually most of the background is filled with designs which, like those of Isfahan, are curvilinear. The colors typical of Nain are cool deep sapphire blues blended with ivory, beige and a pale primrose yellow (see color plate 3). If at first the present-day rugs of Isfahan and Nain seem confusingly alike, just examine the fringes: if they are made of silk, the rug is an Isfahan, and if they are made of cotton, it's a Nain—ninety-nine times out of a hundred.

In the northwest of Persia is the small bustling city of Tabriz which, during the fifteenth century, became a major center for art and learning. The *cloud-band* design, originally imported from China, was first incorporated into Persian patterns by the weavers of Tabriz. Being the nearest Persian city to Europe, Tabriz has

The Isfahan rug these girls are making has a classical Isfahan medallion design

become familiar with most of Persia's rugs, the designs of which the Tabriz weavers frequently borrow. The traditional rug design of Tabriz, however, is a formal curvilinear medallion surrounded by stylized flowers. The lotus blossoms repeated in the borders of the Tabriz rugs resemble turtle shells and are a useful clue in identification.

The coloring of Tabriz rugs varies from pastels to deep rich shades, but the colors are seldom too bright (see color plate 4). The reds, for instance, are usually rust or terra-cotta and the greens are celadon, forest or pistachio rather than emerald. Cream backgrounds with terra-cotta, celadon green and robin's-egg blue medallion designs with turtle-shell borders are typical

Tabriz lotus-blossom design.

of the popular rugs known as Taba-Tabriz (see color plate 5). The name used to refer to the weaving of a particular workshop but it has since become a generalized term.

The wool of the region is comparatively matte and is the strongest in Persia, probably due to the minerals in the water. Besides, in Tabriz they take great care of their sheep. (When I was there, I often saw sheep wearing collars and leashes being taken for walks, although I have a suspicion it was but a short life for the sheep, as a religious holiday was near and they were probably about to be eaten.) Tabriz rugs vary widely in quality. The knotting ranges between 100 and 800 per square inch, with an average knot count of 260. Unfortunately, *tabachi* (wool taken from dead sheep) is sometimes used in the coarser rugs. The warp and weft of most of the Tabriz rugs are made of sturdy cotton. Only the silk or kurk pieces have a silk or fine-grade cotton foundation. Woolen warp and weft threads are very rare.

One of the few examples of undyed Persian rugs, woven in the natural colors of the wools, are those made near Meshed, in a town called Verdose. These rugs have simple, rectilinear patterns, often with plain backgrounds and uncomplicated border designs. These woolen pieces have a low to medium knot count. Nevertheless, they can be exceptionally attractive in contemporary surroundings.

When I refer to a rug as a "Hamadan," I am making a sweeping generalization. Nevertheless, for both the trade and all but the most discriminating expert, the term Hamadan serves perfectly well. Within the Hamadan region are several hundred

The sheep of the Tabriz region are highly regarded.

A Hamadan rug.

villages. The town of Hamadan does produce a few rugs of its own, but its main function is to act as a central trading point for all the other villages. The designs of the area are rectilinear and the vast majority are boldly geometric. The rugs are made of wool knotted onto a firm cotton foundation and the colors of modern Hamadans are usually strong and dark. A zigzag pattern, representing lightning, is typical. The older pieces often contain the soft browns of undyed camel's hair and sharply angled medallions.

TURKEY

The famous Turkish carpets that were so popular here in the 1920s were descendants of the large Ushak carpets woven in Asia Minor from the sixteenth century onward. The later carpets were inferior in design and knotting but retained much of the same coloring of the original Ushaks, large quantities of which were imported to Europe in the eighteenth century. The 1920s carpets were made from wool on a cotton foundation, with a pile of about half an inch (1.5 cm.). They were coarsely woven, usually having no more than 80 knots per square inch. They were also quite large, their average size being fourteen by ten feet (4.27 × 3.05 m.). But their most distinctive feature was their coloring—brilliant scarlet and deep blue with lots of vivid emerald green. Ushaks are still being produced today but they are either bleached or woven in the more popular soft colors.

Turkish rugs were once so popular that the name came to refer to all oriental rugs, just as now the name Persian is, to many people, synonymous with oriental rugs. Turkish rugs are usually made of wool, silk or mercerized cotton on a cotton warp and weft. Their designs are either curvilinear or rectilinear and they are almost always abstract because it is against the Moslem religion to depict any living creature in a lifelike way. The range of tonal effect of rugs made in the towns is medium to light; the effect of the village rugs is darker, but they will include at least two bright colors—a midnight blue rug, for example, with touches of brilliant coral, yellow or gold in the design.

The most common design of Turkish rugs is the prayer arch. When the prayer-arch design consists of multiple mihrabs—the family prayer rug with a mihrab for each member of the family—it is called the *Saph* design. Prayer-arch rugs made in small villages will almost always have a plain center except for a simple, rectilinear design of the holy oil lamp hanging from the

A Saph-design prayer rug.

mihrab. In small towns, the designs are more elaborate: the lamp may be shown as a gaudy chandelier with the two pillars of wisdom rising on either side. Also, a single row of flowers, representing the garden of paradise, may be set at the base of the prayer arch. The Saph design is quite common in these rugs. In more sophisticated town workshops, the design will be further elaborated with "Arabic" script, either in the border or woven into the frame of the arch itself.

Tulips are sometimes used in the design of modern Turkish, often Milas, rugs (their naturally stylized shape is ideally suited to the oriental artistic sense); however, tulips are most likely to be found in antique Turkish rugs. Tulips are Turkish in origin and weren't introduced to Holland until the sixteenth century, as Alexandre Dumas described in *The Black Tulip*. Tulips were reintroduced to Turkey at the end of the seventeenth century, and in the eighteenth century Sultan Ahmed III succumbed to "tulipmania." He was so enthralled by these flowers that the tranquil period at the end of his reign has come to be known as the "tulip period." (Sultan Ahmed liked to entertain his friends by giving extravagant parties. In the summer, these parties were held in the gardens when the tulips were in bloom. An the first stars appeared in the evening sky, oil that had been poured into the cups formed by the tulip petals was lit and the head of each tulip became a tiny enchanting lamp. These tulips, of course, didn't last more than one party, but the sultan had thousands of them to spare.)

In general, Turkish rugs are less sophisticated than Persian rugs, except for those made in the small town of Hereke. Hereke rugs have highly elaborate designs and often gold or silver thread is included in the face of the rug to give it an embossed effect. Hereke rugs are extremely fine quality with a very high knot count (a quite typical knot count will exceed 400 per square inch and finer pieces will exceed 700). These rugs are made entirely of silk and clipped so that the nap is no more than a quarter of an inch deep.

Very few genuine Herekes of dozar and zaranim size can be produced in this small town in a year. Although the name Hereke is given to many rugs made by weavers in the surrounding hamlets, they are inferior in their knotting and design and in the quality of materials used to those woven in the town. These days, even in Hereke itself, not all the glittering metals used to emboss the rugs are pure gold or silver; nevertheless, a true Hereke remains among the finest rugs known (see page 24).

Konya in south-central Turkey (the town that made the rugs Marco Polo described as being the most beautiful in the world) produces only a few coarse rugs now. However, Konya is still well known for its kelims. At one time, all the kelims made in Asia Minor were called Karamani, after the province of Karaman in which Konya is situated.

Kayseri is famous for making most of the mercerized cotton (art silk) rugs. These are the so-called "bazaar" pieces—made to catch the unknowledgeable buyer who hasn't learned to distinguish art silk from real silk rugs. However, not all Kayseris are poor quality; a few of these jewel-colored rugs are beautiful and well made (see color plate 6).

The ancient city of Sparta in southwest Turkey is now called Isparta. In contrast to the rest of Turkey, the weavers of Isparta use the Persian Senneh knot rather than the Turkish Ghiordes knot. Isparta is a collection point for rugs from Turkey and a wide area around it; therefore, a lot of rugs end up being called "Spartas," but only low-grade, commercial rugs are actually woven in the town itself. The weavers will custom-make any pattern and any size of rug; they are also known for their picture rugs.

GREECE

After World War I, many Greeks living in the south of Turkey returned to Greece and settled on the outskirts of Athens. The Anatolian Greeks, as they were called, spoke Turkish and brought their Turkish rug-making skills back with them. The rugs these weavers produced are technically classified as Greek but they are

This person is possibly the only remaining Turkish-Greek weaver.

1. A silk Qum rug showing the garden-of-paradise design.
The turquoise-blue color is peculiar to rugs from the city of Qum.

2. An elegant Isfahan rug. These rugs are among the most finely knotted in Persia.

3. A fine Nain rug with the typical soft coloring of sapphire blues and primrose yellow.

4. A classical, finely woven Tabriz rug with a tear-drop medallion on a Herati-design field.

*5. A pretty example of a Taba-Tabriz rug with typical coloring but
a somewhat unusual garden-of-paradise design.*

6. An "art silk" (mercerized cotton) Turkish Kayseri prayer rug showing the holy lamp suspended from the arch and a pillar of wisdom on either side.

7. A fine example of a nomadic Baluchi prayer rug.

8. *Heriz rugs are also known as Serapis. The balance of the colors with the design in this fine old Heriz (circa 1910) makes it ideally suitable for either a modern or a traditional setting.*

actually Turkish in style. (There are not many of these Turkish-Greek weavers left. When I last visited Greece, I could only find one weaver, supervised by her two elderly aunts who owned the loom and who could no longer weave themselves.)

The modern Greek rugs which are produced in the government workshops are made from wool on a cotton warp and weft. Their colorings are usually soft and pretty—creams, pale turquoise blues and celadon greens are typical. The weavers are also fond of a cool rose pink and a buttery gold. The texture of the rugs is similar to the texture of the Persian Kirmans although their knotting is less fine, with an average of 150 knots per square inch. Their designs are floral, usually similar to a simplified Persian style, and they may be curving or angular. Although they are most attractive pieces, with a nice glossy wool, they are not very hard-wearing because the wool is relatively soft. These Greek rugs are rather expensive despite the fact that they don't have the investment value of the Persian or Turkish pieces.

RUSSIA

The most important period of Russian rugs was during the reign of Catherine the Great, 1762–1796. The first rugs were woven in Kiev for the royal family and have eagle designs in the corners. In general the designs of this period look rather European. They often show vases of flowers or hunting scenes with stags standing at bay and riders galloping across the horizon, all very realistically drawn. These rugs are wool woven on a cotton warp and the knot count is usually not too fine. One of their most striking features is a black background, so look for this to recognize an antique Russian rug.

Modern Russian rugs are perhaps the easiest to identify: they frequently have the initials USSR woven into their borders. The wool may feel harsh (unless it has been chemically treated) and the clip is normally quite short—not more than half an inch (1.5 cm.) deep. These modern rugs are usually of a geometric design and their colors tend to be somber, mostly deep reds and browns with a fair amount of dark blue.

THE CAUCASUS

The rugs from the Caucasus region, on the other hand, have rectilinear designs which are tremendously varied. They often show stylized crabs, beetles or medallions; it is typical to find as many as three or four medallions in a single rug. Borders of Caucasian rugs are elaborately decorated with stars and rosettes

A Caucasian Kasak rug.

and sometimes with a pattern called the *running dog* (similar to the *Greek key* design). The central field may show stylized figures, usually small and often including dogs and chickens. The colors of Caucasian rugs are bright and gay—sky blue is favored as well as red and green. The weave varies from region to region but the average piece contains about 200 knots to the square inch and the fine Shirvans may have as many as 450 knots. Kasaks, on the other hand, have a coarser knotting than Shirvans and simple rectilinear designs. Caucasian rugs are generally small, ranging from five by three feet (1.52 × .91 m.) to nine by six feet (2.74 × 1.83 m.). They are made from wool and are often on a woolen warp as well which gives them a soft, fluffy feeling. (I have yet to see a silk Caucasian, although such rugs are said

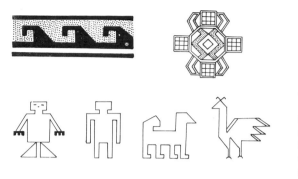

Running-dog design (top left). Kasak crab design (top right). Stylized figures from Caucasian rugs (bottom): men, a dog, and a cock.

to exist.) The designs of Caucasian prayer rugs are always rectilinear with abstract patterns filling the entire rug. The designs are so busy that it is sometimes necessary to study the rug for a few minutes in order to pick out the outline of the prayer arch.

There are, of course, many types of Caucasian rugs aside from Shirvans and Kasaks, although all rugs from the Caucasus tend to share the characteristics mentioned above.

TURKOMAN

The rugs from the Turkoman region of Russia are distinguished by their famous *Bokhara* design. The Bokhara design consists of an octagonal *gul* repeated in rows on the face of the rug. The average size of a Turkoman gul is five inches across by four inches deep (13 × 10 cm.). The design in the center of the gul varies from region to region and is often quartered in different colors. The gul pattern is also called the *elephant's footprint* because the outline of the gul looks like a (small) elephant's footprint. This pattern represents wisdom. The little elongated cross that often divides one gul from another is supposed to be a tarantula—a sign of good luck. The idea is that if you tread on the harmless image of a tarantula woven into a rug, you are less likely to step on a real one. When the Bokhara design contains a thin, usually black, line that connects the rows of guls, it is often referred to as the "Princess" or "Royal Bokhara." This is a retailer's term and should not affect the price of the rug in any way.

The name Bokhara comes from the chief city of the Turkoman region. The area is wild and mountainous and the people of the Turkoman tribes are fiercely independent. Strangers, especially if they come calling in groups, are usually shot at. The Russians tend to feel that the effort needed to take a regular census is not

A Caucasian prayer rug from Daghestan.

worthwhile. Consequently, it is by "reading" and counting the rugs exported to the London market that we can assess how the Turkomans are getting on. Fortunately, collecting these rugs is no problem, for by tradition, anyone wishing to trade does so in the city of Bokhara. This is why all the rugs of the region have come to be called Bokhara, when in fact few, if any, rugs have ever been made there.

The seminomadic tribes of the Turkoman region use rugs to record their personal history. Although the basic design is the gul, each tribe has its own version, as a country has its own flag. The three major tribes are the Tekke, the Salor and the Yomud.

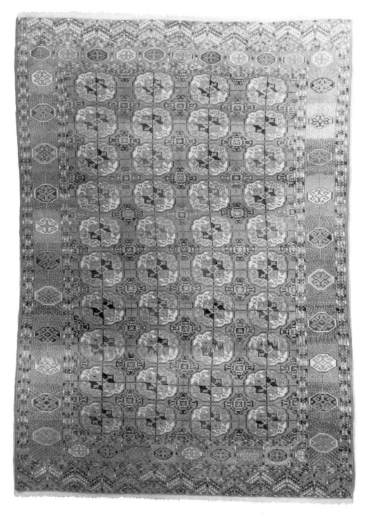

A Tekke Turkoman rug (Bokhara).

As you can see from the drawings, the major differences are in the middles of the guls. It is the middle that is changed when, for instance, a Tekke girl marries into the Yomud tribe. The quarterings of the guls in the rugs that she makes will be a combination of Tekke and Yomud, although the outline of the gul would tactfully follow the Yomud version. (Incidentally, a few Yomuds now live in Persia so it is possible to have a Persian Yomud rug as well as a Turkoman Yomud rug.)

Turkoman rugs, in general, run from a brilliant scarlet through a brownish red to a deep burgundy; frequently, they include white and dark blue and occasionally gold or dark green.

Left to right: Tekke, Salor and Yomud guls.

They usually have a woolen pile woven onto a cotton base, although sometimes the base is made of silk or wool. They come in varying sizes but seldom exceed eleven by eight feet (3.35 × 2.44 m.).

The *hatchlu* design used in the Turkoman region is a large cross but it has no connection with the Christian religion. The cross symbolizes the doorposts of a house (a sturdy house with solid doorposts is a beautiful thing in the eyes of a wandering nomad) and these rugs mark the doorways of the nomads' tents.

Baluchi rugs are made by nomads who wander through the Turkoman region, along the Persian and Afghanistan borders and down to West Pakistan. The Afghan town of Herat is a major collecting point for Baluchi rugs. The predominant colors of Baluchi rugs are dark blue or blue-black, rust-reds and a bluish mauve which gives the pile a purplish sheen (see color plate 7). Occasionally, they will use touches of cream, ivory or camel. A few pieces are also made in a wide variety of colors, including vermilion, light blue, green, yellow, copper and violet. The kelim ends of Baluchi rugs are often highly decorated (this is peculiar to them) and sometimes the kelims have an "over-fringe" as an extension of the colors of the rug.

Baluchi designs are simple rectilinear patterns, mostly abstract guls, stylized trees and rosette-type flowers. They also use allover designs of stars, angular botehs, stylized animals, birds and small chickens. The *running-dog* and the *angular-wave* designs are typically used in the borders of the rugs. The most common size for these rugs is five by three feet (1.52 × .91 m.), or zaranim, especially for prayer rugs. Larger pieces are made but they are always long and thin because the nomadic Baluchis use a horizontal loom. Because of this loom, the rugs are often irregular in shape (as explained in Chapter 2). The wool is lustrous, tough and resilient and is woven onto a woolen warp and weft, which makes the rugs feel supple. The side cords are typically wide and flat and they are often bound with goat or other animal hair. The mihrabs of the prayer rugs are either sharply pointed or

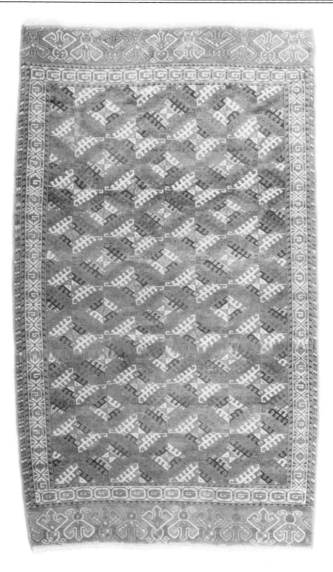

A Yomud Turkoman rug (Bokhara).

drawn as a definite square. Occasionally, the outline of a hand with fingers spread will be woven on either side of the square mihrab.

The Persian town of Meshed has lent its name to a few Baluchis who have chosen to settle on the outskirts of the town. The difference between the work of the Meshed Baluchis (the settled villagers) and the nomadic Baluchis is that the Meshed Baluchis weave finer rugs with a shorter pile. Their rugs are

A hatchlu-design rug.

almost exclusively made in deep reds, blues and beiges, with occasional touches of cream. The Meshed Baluchi rugs have a formal look and are usually free of the engaging irregularities of weave, coloring and shape so often found in the rugs of the Baluchi nomads.

AFGHANISTAN

Probably due to the early nomadic journeyings of the tribes of the Turkoman region, the Bokhara design spread east into Afghanistan. However, Afghan Bokharas are easy to recognize because their guls are typically much larger than Turkoman guls.

A nomadic Baluchi prayer rug with a stylized tree-of-life design.

The average Afghan gul measures seven to twelve inches (18 to 31 cm.), as compared with the four- to five-inch (10 to 13 cm.) Turkoman guls. Again, the center is quartered, with linear designs included in the quarterings.

The rugs of Afghanistan have a limited color range. They are generally deep red with blue-black designs. Occasionally white, dark green, or both are added. Afghan rugs may include jute in

Afghan gul.

their warp and weft, but the good ones are made on a cotton warp and weft with a woolen pile. These rugs come in all sizes, with an average knot count of 150; it is unusual to find one with a knot count above 300 per square inch. A few rugs are woven in a golden yellow color but, sadly, as I have described in Chapter 3, many red rugs are chemically bleached to simulate the golden color.

Afghanistan prayer rugs are similar to those of the Baluchis, although the Afghans tend to be more coarsely woven than the Baluchis and their designs are more pronounced. Their guls are nearly always true octagons with the sides squared off into bold angular patterns.

ROMANIA AND BULGARIA

Romania is most famous for its kelim weaving. Modern Romanian kelims are not expensive and are usually reversible and well made. They often have a sort of hairy look about them due to the use of mill-spun yarn, which is not particularly suitable for the weaving of kelims. Old pieces are often finely woven from hand-spun yarn and so are smoother in appearance. The designs of Romanian kelims (flat-woven pieces) are rectilinear and often floral. Because the weavers were fond of using deep reds and blues, the colors of the old pieces are often quite somber. However, in the modern kelims, brighter colors and more variation have been introduced to please Western tastes.

In 1947, large workshops were constructed in many parts of Romania to produce rugs. These rugs are wool on a cotton warp and weft and, as opposed to the kelims, are very sturdy. The wool is lustrous and hard-wearing and the pile is half an inch or more in length. The knot counts range from coarse, about 80 knots, to fine, 300 knots per square inch. Sizes range from about three by two feet (.91 × .61 m.) up to fourteen by ten feet (4.27 × 3.05 m.) or larger.

Designs are taken from the traditional Persian designs,

An old Afghan rug, circa 1900.

especially the curvilinear patterns. The medallion design is one of the most popular and the small animals and birds of which Persia is so fond are also quite often found in these rugs. The tonal effect of Romanian rugs is generally light to medium and their colors are very much attuned to Western tastes. A light golden beige is perhaps the most typical part of their color schemes, along with gold, champagne, pink, blue, green and muted red. The price of these rugs is about half that of their Persian counterparts. They are a sensible choice for people who want a hard-wearing, handmade oriental rug but who don't want to spend a lot of money on it.

Bulgarian rugs are very similar to Romanian rugs in that they use Persian designs. Bulgarian rugs are also made from wool on a fine cotton foundation and their white fringes show neatly at either end. Although their wool is of good quality, the gloss is less apparent on Bulgarian rugs because the clip is much shorter (half an inch or less) and the colors are paler than in Romanian rugs. The most typical color of a Bulgarian rug is ivory, together with a pale rose pink or turquoise blue. The best Bulgarian pieces have a higher knot count (about 400 per square inch) than most Romanian rugs one sees in the stores and they cost more: i.e., a Bulgarian rug will cost about two-thirds the price of its Persian counterpart.

INDIA

Some of the most famous Indian rugs take their name from the town of Agra (where the Taj Mahal is located) which, in the early seventeenth century, had a large jail to which long-term prisoners were sent. To keep their charges occupied, the jailers decided—practically and profitably—that the prisoners should weave rugs. The original Agra carpets are often large and their colors are soft, frequently due to fading.

Agra still produces rugs, but these days they are made outside the prison. Modern Agras resemble the rugs made in Pakistan (see below) except that they use the Persian designs instead of the Bokhara design. They are woven with very soft wool and, in spite of being on a cotton warp and weft, are floppy because they are coarsely knotted with an average count of 170 knots per square inch. Their fringes are white and the colors of their curvilinear designs tend to be vivid but not necessarily overly bright, as they follow the general colorings of the Persian designs they copy.

The thick, heavy modern Indian rugs are among the most reasonable in price and the most popular in America. They have a deep pile, usually with no gloss because of the type of wool used. Jute may be used in the foundation threads. The designs are floral or plain, following the "French-Chinese" style (discussed below), and the colors in the best examples are pastel. Many of the rugs have a pale background with designs woven in soft pinks, greens, golds and turquoise. The inferior pieces can be distinguished by harsh colors in their designs, often including deep claret.

The fluffy white Indian rugs, typical of the town of Mirzapur, often show the Aubusson design: heavy floral borders and medallions with a quartered medallion in each corner. These pieces come in all sizes and are usually quite coarsely woven. If

An Indian Aubusson-design rug.

you are choosing this type of Indian rug, be sure that the pile is made from machine-spun yarn. The hand-spun yarn will "fluff." Don't let a salesman convince you that this fluffing is temporary—it's not. The wool will continue to fluff year after year, so that you will be vacuuming your rug until, quite literally, nothing is left but the cotton warp and weft. Machine-spun yarn gives a smoother, more groomed appearance to the rug and, more important, it will not fluff like the hand-spun yarn. However, *some* fluffing must be expected for the first three months or so; this is simply excess fibers coming away. The machine-spun wool rugs may be more expensive, but these Indian rugs are so reasonably priced to begin with that this is another reason for you to buy the best.

Rugs from the Vale of Kashmir in India have elaborate floral Persian designs. Their most distinguishing features are the high gloss of the woolen pile and the sturdy white fringe of the cotton warp. Occasionally, they are made of a low-grade silk or mercerized cotton. In general, Kashmir rugs are well made, with an average knot count of about 350, although they are not as strong as the Persian rugs because softer wool is used. Kashmirs range in tone from medium to light, with a distinctive deep green color with a bluish yellow glow appearing in most of them. They come in small to medium sizes—five by three feet (1.52 × .91 m.) to about ten by seven feet (3.05 × 2.13 m.). Good Kashmirs are attractive pieces and their designs are so similar to the Persian ones that unless you remind yourself to look for the gloss of the wool and the white fringe, it is easy to confuse Kashmirs with Persians.

PAKISTAN

Pakistan produces very finely woven rugs made of wool with a high gloss. This is particularly true of the Pakistani Bokhara rugs—except for those made in 1930 when Pakistan first began to use the Bokhara design. These early pieces, like most of the subsequent ones, followed the original Turkoman Bokhara designs and they were finely knotted. Unfortunately, the wool that was used to make these rugs came from discarded British army socks and the rugs fell to pieces after a very short time. This gave Pakistan a rather poor reputation, from which it was slow to recover.

The present-day rugs are made from high-quality wools, often including merino wool imported from Australia. One of the most distinguishing features of a Pakistani rug is the high gloss of its wool. The wool is so glossy that the colors really appear to change as you walk from one end of the rug to the other, as though it were made of silk.

The Bokhara design reached Pakistan via the wandering Baluchis who liked and copied the elephant's-footprint idea. The Pakistani Bokharas are often remarkably similar to the Turkoman Bokharas, but they are made in a wider variety of color combinations, ranging through ivory and pale blue to deep ruby red, chocolate and even royal purple. Pakistani rugs have very wide, elaborate borders and about three inches of sturdy white cotton fringe from the warp showing at either end. If you see a rug with a Bokhara design, a high knot count of about 350 knots per square inch, a very high gloss and a bright white cotton fringe, the rug was almost certainly made in Pakistan and should be less than half the price of its Turkoman counterpart.

CHINA

It is widely believed that because the language of the Chinese is characterized by a limited number of spoken words, a rich language of symbols has evolved. Most of the Chinese symbols have religious origins. The early Chinese Taoist religion was deeply concerned not only with the quality of life but with the length of life as well. Among the many Taoist symbols for longevity, a surprising example is the butterfly. Another symbol is a pair of cranes—a long and happy life. The Buddhist religion also strongly influenced Chinese pictorial symbolism. Fo, the maned lion often shown with a round ball beneath its paw, was originally a Buddhist symbol. Fo was widely adopted by the Chinese artists but has, for them, no religious significance. Among the many Chinese symbols are:

Fir tree—everlasting
Infinite knot—never-ending happiness
Lotus—purity; lotus bud—all-powerful
Fishes—plenty
Goldfish—deliverance; also a happy marriage
Peony—material success
Scepter—success in all things
Sword—supernatural power
Vase—wisdom or peace
Wheel—law, prayers or prayer wheel, often depicted as being on fire
Swastika—joy and great happiness
Bat—happiness and good luck
Umbrella—dignity
Pair of Mandarin ducks—faithful and happy marriage
Waves—the sea; circles—quiet water
Coin—money, wealth

The fine arts (civilized living) are represented by:

Harp—sometimes referred to as a lute
Chessboard (chess is believed to have been invented by the Chinese)
Two paintings—drawn as two rolled-up scrolls
Book—drawn as a rectangular block often accompanied by paint brushes

Another well-known Chinese symbol is the Yin and Yang. This represents opposites: active/passive; dark/light; high/low. The Tao, the all-pervading cosmos.

When you are deciphering the Chinese "picture" language, do remember that the combination of symbols is important. For example, a grasshopper (government employee) sitting on a chrysanthemum (permanency), with a deer (affluence) standing nearby, would express a wish for a good job on a permanent basis that pays well. Also, remember that a symbol may have more than one meaning: e.g., a deer means affluence but a stag means long life; a butterfly means long life but it may also mean a happy marriage; the bamboo plant means meek or bashful but, because its leaves resemble paper, it can also mean famous (because the way of being forever remembered is to be written about).

The most famous of China's legendary beasts is called Dragon-lung. This dragon is always male. If he is a blue-green dragon, he is known as Lord of the East—spring, rain, sunrise and all light. The next most important among the many Chinese dragons and beasts—360 to be precise—is Feng-huang, the phoenix, Dragon-lung's female equivalent. She was the royal bird and symbolizes the opposite qualities of Dragon-lung:

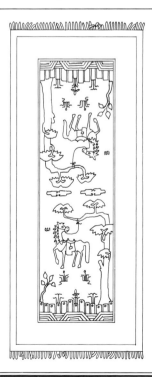

Drawing of a nineteenth-century Chinese picture rug from Suiyuan, showing a horse under a tree.

A Chinese rug, circa 1800, with "foliage" dragons and a peony border.

whereas he stands for sunrise and all light, she represents sunset and darkness—but not in a negative way. Feng-huang symbolizes the more down-to-earth side of life; for example, sexual union, nurturing and caring for the family. When Dragon-lung is shown with Feng-huang, this is thought to bring blessings, especially if the wishing pearl (a flaming multicolored sphere) is included in the design.

There are also four little dragons. They are t'ien-lung, the sky dragon; ti-lung, the earth dragon; shên-lung, the spirit dragon; and a very fierce dragon called fu-ts'ang-lung, whose job is guarding treasure. If fu-ts'ang-lung has five toes, he is the guardian of the royal treasure at the court and has no business with anyone except the emperor.

The colors of the traditional early Chinese rugs were mostly deep blue, light blue and cream, but beige, rose and pale green were also used. When a bright golden yellow was included, this piece was meant for the exclusive use of the emperor.

During the early 1900s, China began exporting rugs to the Western world and the European markets demanded that anything Chinese should look "Chinese." So the traditional designs were altered to include little temples, elephants, oxen and other symbols—all looking typically "Chinese." In 1930, the Western markets wanted an additional style and the fashionable French Aubusson and Savonnerie designs began to be copied. These had elaborate floral patterns with heavily decorated borders and central medallions. The modern Chinese rugs you see in the stores today are variations on these designs.

Modern Chinese rugs are made in almost every color combination imaginable, including rugs with pure black backgrounds. Light pinks, golds, greens and other pastel shades are used for the designs. You may even find an occasional dragon in the modern Chinese rug, although he is more likely to be surrounded by flowers instead of his traditional cloud of smoke.

The modern Chinese pieces have a very deep pile. The designs are deeply embossed by a skilled cutter who, using a short knife, carves around the edges of the design to give it a three-dimensional appearance. The pile is then given a high gloss with a nonbleaching chemical wash. Because the knotting of these modern pieces is rather coarse, the depth of the pile is important in order to give these rugs their compact appearance. Today, the pile of the best Chinese rugs is five-eighths of an inch long. Rugs are also made with four-eighths-inch and three-

Drawing of Feng-huang, the dragon-phoenix, and Dragon-lung.

A modern silk-washed woolen Chinese rug, showing the Aubusson design.

eighths-inch pile. These thinner pieces look similar to the "90-line, ⅝" rugs, which is how we describe them in the trade (or "silk-washed," as the retailers sometimes call them), but they are of an inferior quality and should only cost about half the amount of the thicker pieces. (The term "90-line" refers to the number of knots, counting downward for ten inches [25 cm.]. This description originated when the Chinese were first doing business with the West in the early 1920s. They needed a commercial way of categorizing the various qualities of rugs and thought they would simplify the Persian system of measuring knots per square inch, by measuring knots per square foot. However, the Chinese thought there were only ten inches in a foot, so 90-line really means ninety lines in ten inches.)

Rug-weaving has become so highly organized in China and such vast quantities of rugs are being produced that modern Chinese rugs have little investment potential. They are the only oriental rugs that lose their value once they have been used— like a new car once it has been driven around the block. However, the reproduction Chinese rugs that are woven in the antique style, using the original colors and symbols, are well worth collecting.

The majority of Chinese rugs are made from wool on a cotton warp and weft. This is true of the antique as well as the modern rugs. Silk rugs are produced in the province of Shantung, famous for its silk. These silk rugs have a coarser texture than Persian silk rugs; this is due to fewer knots per square inch and not to an inferior-quality silk. Chinese silk rugs are generally woven in the antique style, and in the case of the inexpensive ones, they will have a gaudy golden fringe added to either end, although the actual warp threads will have been made from cotton. A recent development in Chinese rug-making is the copying of traditional Persian designs and colorings. These rugs are woven in pure silk and often have a knot count of over 500 knots per square inch.

Occasionally, you may come across an antique Chinese saddle cover, usually lined with soft felt. Their designs are the ancient symbols, often including one similar to the Greek key design around the outer border. Saddle covers may have a dark blue or red background with the design worked in beige or nut brown. Because few of these saddle covers have survived, they are highly prized.

Antique Chinese saddle rug showing the infinite-knot design.

Left: A Tibetan pillar rug with
various Buddhist symbols. Right:
A Tibetan temple rug. The medallions are formed from peony and
cloud designs.

TIBET

The Tibetans were not too concerned with the symbolism of the pictorial language of China but they liked to use the Chinese designs in their rugs. One of the Tibetan weavers' favorite designs is the dragon (any dragon). They are also fond of weaving circular medallions, particularly for their meditation mats which are approximately two feet (.61 m.) square. Occasionally, several squares are joined together, presumably to accommodate a row of monks.

Following the Chinese occupation of Tibet, a considerable number of refugees went to Europe. Although they immediately began weaving, their rugs lack the charm and gaiety of the original ones. They are made solely for commercial reasons. Instead of using the traditional colors and designs of Tibet, the rugs are woven in "Western" color schemes and the designs are coarsened versions of the most popular Chinese motifs.

NORTH AFRICA

Modern North African rugs, which decorate the bazaars so colorfully, are often made with poor-quality wool and are so loosely woven that they can wear out very quickly. They often have as many as seven rows of knots before a single weft thread is included. These rugs have a woolen pile, usually cut to about half an inch long, with a cotton warp and weft. The outer edges have flat side cords made of wool. The colors are quite garish; the Moroccan weavers especially are fond of crude reds and yellows, although today it is possible to find Moroccan rugs undyed, woven in the natural colors of the wools: simple creams, greys, browns and blacks. These color combinations also appear in the few rugs that are made in Libya. The Libyan rugs are a much better quality than the new Moroccan pieces.

The designs of modern North African rugs are, unlike the old rugs of that region, quite simple. Antique Moroccan rugs in particular have far more ornate and intricate designs, with a typical soft yellow color or pale mauve. The wool of the antique rugs was of a much better quality than is used today, although the knotting was never very dense. The warp and weft threads were either wool or goat's hair. If a rug has a cotton warp or weft, you may be sure that it is a modern "antique." Genuine antique North African rugs are very valuable pieces and much sought after. If you consider buying a modern North African rug, be sure to read my discussion of bargaining in Chapter 8 first.

EGYPT

In Europe in the early eighteenth century, rugs were generally considered far too precious to walk on. They were hung on walls to keep out drafts and draped over tables. The Egyptians made some pieces specially designed for the European market woven in the shape of a cross for covering tables: the central square area of the rug covered the tabletop and the arms of the cross fell tidily on each side.

Mamluk rugs are among the most famous of the Egyptian pieces. They were woven in the fifteenth and sixteenth centuries and many fine examples are preserved in museums. After the Ottomans conquered Egypt, the Mamluk patterns with their narrow medallions were gradually replaced by the Turkish designs popular in the Ottoman court at the time.

Egypt ceased producing noteworthy original rugs at the end of the eighteenth century. In the modern pieces, woven in Heluan, the pile is approximately the same length as that of the modern Kirmans whose designs they copy, as they do many of the other Persian patterns. Unfortunately, the colors chosen in which to weave these patterns are often both vibrant and crude. However, occasionally, when they are soft and pretty, the Egyptian rugs compare well with some of the models that they have copied. This is especially true in the case of Kirmans. The copies, with their central "medallion design-with-corners" (with decorated borders and corners), the wool used, together with the style and "look" of the weave (the knotting), can be devastatingly deceptive—to the novice and the experienced buyer alike. Only if you remember that these copies do exist and so compare them with the original (physically at first and mentally as you become more expert) can you be absolutely confident that your Persian Kirman is not an Egyptian in disguise.

An Isfahan rug with a one-way garden-of-paradise design.

CHAPTER FIVE

Windows to Walk On

For most of us, home is neither a historic castle porched high on a hill, nor is it a chilly cave dug into the hillside. Home is more likely to be a boxlike structure, subdivided into rectangular shapes and frequently painted white. Onto this unlikely space we try to stamp our personalities; so we decorate. These days almost everything is mass-produced and almost anything we buy will have been bought by many other people who are also decorating their spaces. We may choose our living-room furniture from among hundreds of styles and even more varieties of coverings. We may spend a small fortune on custom-made draperies and wall-to-wall carpeting. Yet when the room is finished, we may find it disappointingly similar to that of our neighbor. What we need is something that will give our own room originality and personality. What we need is an oriental rug.

Oriental rugs come in so many styles that this is one time when you really can have exactly what you want. Often the hardest part is deciding what it is you do want. Should the rug be grandly elegant, or should it be a more practical piece that can withstand a boisterous family life and still look its best when you entertain? Perhaps you want a rug that is meant just for you, well protected in a child-free and pet-free corner of your home that is especially your own. It is important to answer these questions before you even consider trying out a rug in your home.

SIZE

The most natural mistake people make when buying an oriental rug is to buy too large a rug. We are so used to wall-to-wall carpeting that it is easy to forget that an oriental rug is more akin to "art for the floor" than it is to regular machine-made carpeting. As with most art, your oriental needs a spatial frame to allow it to be seen properly. The safest general rule to go by is, the more space you allow to frame your rug, the more beautiful it will look.

For a room-sized piece that is to lie on a polished floor you need a minimum of space: one foot (31 cm.) on either side of the carpet and one foot, four inches (41 cm.) at either end. The extra four inches (10 cm.) accounts for the fact that rugs are seldom measured to include their fringes. However, if the rug is to lie on top of wall-to-wall carpeting, you will need more space. I recommend a minimum of two feet, six inches (1.68 m.) all around; otherwise the effect will be overcrowded. There is too little difference in texture between the oriental and the carpet for our eyes to register the separation of the two surfaces. (If your floor is not wood or totally plain wall-to-wall carpeting, you will have special considerations and may need advice from an interior designer. However, later in this chapter I shall give you one or two possible solutions to this problem.)

When deciding whether you want a full room-size rug or a much smaller piece, begin by taking a careful look at the proportions of your room. How large is it? (Exclude the alcoves and, in the case of L-shaped rooms, the short side of the L.) Does the room have a high ceiling? How big are the windows? Do they dominate the room? Are they modern and unobtrusive or are they more like those of the last century with the glass divided into small squares or diamond shapes? Are the windows accented by broad sills or window seats? What style are the door and window frames? Are there architectural details that stand out, such as an elaborate cornice? If you live in an old house it is worth remembering that wall-to-wall carpeting is a relatively recent idea; old houses were built when the only choice for floor coverings, apart from homemade rugs, was oriental rugs. If one of the features in your room is a fireplace, does it have an important, obvious design? Is it built of stone or brick? Does it have a substantial mantelpiece?

If the answer to any of these proportion questions is yes, then you will probably need at least one full-size oriental rug so that your room will be in balance. If you also want a few small rugs about the place, that is fine; but a room has to be balanced to feel aesthetically comfortable and the expanse of the large oriental will give you your foundation for design. However, there is one practical consideration: I suggest that the largest rug you consider be fourteen by ten feet (4.27 × 3.05 m.) or even twelve by nine feet (3.66 × 2.74 m.). If you change houses, these two sizes will fit into the average room, whereas chances are that a twenty-five-by-eighteen-foot (7.6 × 5.49 m.) rug will not. Well-chosen oriental rugs have a way of becoming part of the family and it would be a shame to be faced with the choice of getting rid of the rug or rebuilding your new home.

Size is especially important if you are buying a rug for your dining room. Make sure that you choose one that is wide enough: allow for the width of the table plus two feet (61 cm.) on either side for the chairs to be pulled back. For example, if your table is three feet (91 cm.) wide, you should get a rug that is at least seven feet (2.13 m.) wide. It can be very irritating if the two back legs of a chair constantly catch on the edge of a rug that is too narrow. It's not very good for the rug either.

If you want to use your rug in front of the sofa in your living room, place it so that one edge runs parallel to the seat of the sofa. The rug should be at least one foot (31 cm.) longer than the sofa to balance the height of the sofa. If the style of the sofa is a heavy one, such as a Chesterfield, allow at least two feet (61 cm.) so that the rug passes the sofa by one foot (31 cm.) at either end. If you use this arrangement, try to leave a clear frame on the other three sides of the rug. Your sofa and rug will then form a unified group and help to set each other off.

STYLE AND COLOR

When you have decided on the approximate size that your rug should be, it is time to look at the scale of your furnishings. Is the majority of your furniture made up of large or small pieces? Does its design tend towards being delicate or substantial? What kinds of patterns are there already in the room— on the draperies, for instance, or on upholstered furniture? Try to determine whether your room leans more towards bold contemporary patterns or softer traditional ones.

Next, assess the textures you have used: smooth velvets, silks and satins should be classified as traditional, while burlaps, corks, rough linen, or woolen finishes like tweed would be regarded as modern. Colors should be considered in the same way. Dark or pastel colors are generally traditional. Vivid colors such as lime green or bright pink are usually contemporary.

A Yallahmeh rug.

Broadly speaking, strong contrasts produce a contemporary effect (such as orange with black or purple with yellow), whereas gentle blends of color (soft blues with golds) create a more traditional effect. Strongly geometric rugs like the new Sinkiangs (China) or Yallahmehs (Persia) with their clear colors and designs suit contemporary rooms; the softly curving Shah Abbas designs of Kashan and Isfahan look good in traditional settings. Whether your room is modern or traditional in style, at least one of the colors in the room should appear in the oriental rug that you choose. This will ensure that the rug locks into the room and becomes a unified part of your decor.

DURABILITY

After you have narrowed down your choice of rugs by size, style and color, there is one more very important question to answer: Is your rug going to be basically decorative or will it have to stand up to hard wear and tear? If you do not have to be concerned with the durability of the rug, silk rugs are worth considering because they are so beautiful. However, they are not strong and really should be hung on a wall or used in a bedroom or in an area of the living room where they will seldom be walked on.

Some years ago, a client brought me what had once been a remarkably fine silk rug. She had used it in her hallway for five years. Although in places the rug was undamaged, where the traffic pattern had been there was a foot-wide (31 cm.) strip with no pile left and no design visible. The rug was worthless; to restore it would have cost more than buying a new piece.

Another client of mine, a writer, had a silk Kashan rug under his desk for twenty-five years. Naturally enough, the area where his feet had rested was almost worn out. But the really serious damage had been done by the legs of his chair. Each time he pushed or pulled the chair to move it, the legs dug into the rug. There were places where the rug had been sliced into thin ribbons. If that silk Kashan had been carefully looked after, its value today would be about $20,000 at auction.

So if you intend to use your rug, it is much safer to avoid the silk ones and choose instead the much more durable woolen ones. In the course of normal wear, these woolen rugs simply become more beautiful. The pile develops such a sheen that it looks almost like silk. As long as the rug has been properly woven and its wool has not been mistreated, it really is true that the more you walk on a woolen rug, the more beautiful it becomes. However, the tread pattern should be kept as even as possible (see Chapter 6). Many people find it useful to place their woolen oriental on top of their wall-to-wall carpet in the hardest-wear spots: in front of a door, in front of French windows and even on the stairs, where a good handmade woolen oriental will outlast a machine-made carpet by at least two generations.

It is generally agreed that the most enduring wool in all Persia comes from the Tabriz region. Perhaps it is minerals in the water that are transmitted to the sheep through their feed;

or perhaps it is that Tabriz lies in the northwest of Iran where the weather is severe so that the sheep develop hardy coats. In any case, the fleece from sheep bred in Tabriz produces the sturdiest wool and rugs from Tabriz are ideal for areas of heavy traffic.

MIXING AND MATCHING

I am frequently asked whether it is all right to put old or antique rugs with new furniture. There is no hard and fast rule about this and my answer is, yes, of course it can be done. Just be sure that the contrast between the rug and the furniture is sufficiently strong so that the rug doesn't end up looking shabby. Putting an antique rug in the same setting as, for instance, glass furniture can look marvelous. The simple uncluttered lines of contemporary furniture can be used to highlight old rugs. (See color plate 8.)

A friend of mine decorated her Manhattan apartment entirely in shades of white and ivory. Even the wall-to-wall carpeting was ivory, and the only color in the room was the green of her plants. A brass-edged glass coffee table holding a crystal vase with white daisies in it stood between two contemporary ivory-colored velvet sofas. Beneath the table lay her glowing coral antique Saruk (Persia) rug. The effect of the Saruk's single pool of subtle color on the almost totally white scene was superb.

The reverse situation—using new oriental rugs with old or antique furniture—can also work. It works especially well if you avoid bright colors and choose either pale-toned rugs or rugs that are dark and richly colored. You can often find pale-toned rugs among the pieces produced in Kashmir and Pakistan. For a richly toned rug you might look for a pigeon's-blood Afghan with the guls woven in a midnight blue (this looks exceptionally good with oak). Whichever new rugs you choose to go with old furniture, the wool should be glossy enough to link up with the polished surfaces of your antiques. If the fringes of your rug are too white and contrasting, you can tone them down with a coffee or tea rinse (see Chapter 6). This will help to blend the rug in with its surroundings.

Another question that is often raised is whether or not different types of oriental rugs should be put together in the same room. The answer depends on just how different the rugs are. To use rugs in combination, they should have at least two characteristics in common—design, texture, or color— so they will be linked together. As a general rule, it is always wise to avoid jarring differences when mixing and matching oriental rugs.

One of the most important characteristics of any rug is its design. When you mix rugs, choose either rectilinear-design rugs or curvilinear-design rugs. If the two types are mixed, they tend to detract from one another. (As I have explained in Chapter 2, rectilinear rugs are usually produced in the tribes or villages.) However, there are a few exceptions and the curvilinear Persian-garden design so often made in Qum is one of them. The series of squares from which this design is made goes perfectly with rectilinear rugs; yet the interior design of each of the squares is woven so delicately that, contrary to the rules, it looks equally harmonious with curvilinear rugs.

Texture is another aspect of rugs and it varies from "wildly woolly" to "smooth as silk." While the rougher wools are attractive in their own right, they will only look badly made when seen next to velvet Isfahans or sleek Pakistan rugs.

Color and tone are also important when mixing rugs, particularly if you intend to put, for example, a Turkish rug next to a Persian rug. When you are considering buying a piece that has a high sheen, always remember to look at it from both ends. As with velvet, the pile of rugs is set on an angle so that when you look *into* the pile you will see one color and when you look *along* the pile the color will often appear to be many shades lighter. The length of the pile of the two rugs should be roughly the same, and so should the sheen of their wool.

To see if the tones of the two rugs are balanced, lay them side by side and stand back a little to look at them, half closing your eyes. Forget the colors for a moment and look for the depth of tone. If one rug is much lighter or darker than the other, the combination is not going to work. Be sure to do this test in daylight so that you will get a true reading of the tonal balance. Try to be sure also that the rugs share one or two colors of the same tone. For example, they might each contain a little turquoise or gold or orange—any definite touch of color will help to pull the rugs together to form a unified scheme. Also bear in mind that the size difference in rugs should not be too extreme. A room-sized rug is as powerful a decoration as a very large painting. Most people would hesitate before putting a tiny picture next to an enormous one, and the same principle applies to rugs.

In general, a safe way to mix rugs is to choose pieces that come from the same country, have similar styles of design (the styles should match—rectilinear rugs with rectilinear rugs and curvilinear with curvilinear) and are approximately the same age. However, antique rugs tend to cost more than new ones. If you would like to add to your collection of rugs but would rather not spend the money to get another antique, go ahead and buy a new one. Just be sure to follow the guidelines I have given above when blending a new rug with your antique rugs. Take special care, however, to avoid choosing very shiny new rugs; you want to match the patina of your antique rug, not outdo it. Bright white fringes on a new rug are not a problem because they can be toned down with the coffee/tea rinse. Try to avoid "antique-washed" rugs. They almost never look right and are not a shortcut to the suggestions above.

If you follow these guidelines you should not have to worry about matching up the number of knots per square inch in your various rugs. They should lie happily enough together, and you may find that their knot counts will be similar. If they are not, it is not important. Few of your friends are going to compare the backs of your rugs; it is the general effect that people will notice.

So that the effect will be as harmonious as possible, try to leave some distance between the old rugs and the new one. Three feet (91 cm.) is usually fine. Also, it is a good idea to place your new rug where it will catch the sun. The strong light will help to weather it and make it more compatible with your old rugs.

Within these limits, you can feel quite confident in mixing rugs that have been made hundreds of miles and hundreds of year apart. And the result will probably be much more interesting and lively than if you had spent many weeks and dollars searching for exactly matching pieces.

FINDING A RUG FOR YOUR ROOM

If you are bored with the decor of your home, yet feel unable to face the upheaval and expense of throwing out everything, including the children, and starting all over again, try to change just one room at a time. Remembering the points I made earlier in this chapter, go to your nearest rug store. Try to select a rug that you think will suit the room you have chosen to work with. Explain to the salesperson that you would like to borrow the rug for a few days because you're not sure whether it's right for you. If you are dealing with a large department store there should be no difficulty in arranging this. If you have an account with the store, the rug will be charged to your account. If you don't have an account, you will have to pay for the rug. In either case, be sure that the receipt is marked "sale or return" or "on approval only." The store must then agree to refund your money.

If you go to one of the small specialist oriental-rug stores, it is more than likely that the owner will lend you the rug on an informal basis. He may insist on delivering it to be sure that you live at the address you have given because oriental rugs are valuable items and the store owner will want to protect himself. Most specialist stores will lend rugs to people because they are fully aware that an oriental rug will dramatically transform a room. They know that once you have seen a rug in your room it will be very hard to be content with plain wall-to-wall carpeting.

The object of this exercise is to show you how an oriental rug will affect your room. At this stage you need not be concerned about a particular color or design. Just go ahead and choose a rug that appeals to you. Remember that the first rug you select to borrow may not be the one you decide to buy.

Now that you have the rug home, I suggest that you set it aside for a moment and go back to the drawing board. You need to decide where the main focus of your room is and where it could be. The focal point of a room could be the fireplace, the French windows (especially if they look onto a pretty view) or your favorite piece of furniture. Try out the oriental in each of these locations until you find the place that seems just right for you. If the room seems to have no focal point, the rug itself can provide this.

Having decided how you want the rug to be positioned, roll it up again. With pencil and paper in hand, take a careful look at your room. Note the main color theme of draperies, walls, floor, upholstery. Don't go into detail; you want the overall color effect. If the large sofas are blue but the occasional chair is rose, ignore the chair and just write "blue." If the draperies or walls are patterned, stand well back and look at them with half-closed eyes. Decide which single color they appear to be and write it down.

What you are trying to find out is which of the three primary colors you have used to decorate your room. The primary colors are red, blue and yellow. Pinks and rich browns go under the heading of red; cool lilacs, celadon and forest greens would be counted as blue; lime greens, golds and true oranges are in the yellow group. After you have noted all the main colors in your room, look at your list. You should have used one, at the most two, primary colors. A room that has all three colors looks messy because the eye is constantly confused by them. However,

A typical "antique style" Chinese rug.

different shades of one or two color groups are fine; black and white should not be counted.

Suppose you discover that you have used only one primary color in your room—blue, for instance. If you want to retain the calm atmosphere that this produces, I suggest you choose an oriental that, in its coloring, contains only blues. An example of this would be a blue and creamy white "antique-style" Chinese rug. Or you might prefer to give your room a lift by adding a second primary color, perhaps yellow. Remember that yellow includes all the shades from sunshine yellow to lemon to primrose

A nineteenth-century Chinese rug.

to gold. Persian Kirman rugs are often woven in blues and golds, and the people of Nain produce some marvelous deep blue and primrose combinations in their work.

If you want to give your room sparkling vitality, try adding a touch of the contrasting color to your basic primary. In the case of blue, this is orange; in the case of red, it is green; for yellow, the contrasting color is purple. Try to make sure that the rug you choose contains both the contrasting and the primary color. It will then become part of your overall scheme and you will have the added effect of seeing the colors bounce off each other. You can find blue/orange combinations in rugs from the Tabriz region in the north of Iran and all the way south to the rugs of Pakistan and Kashmir.

Where I have suggested double color combinations in rugs, I do not mean that the rugs are made in two colors exclusively. With the exception of the Afghans and the "antique-style" Chinese rugs, rugs usually contain touches of many other colors. I am referring to their two predominant colors, one of which will probably be the background color.

If, when you consult your list, you find that you have already used two primary colors, I suggest that you definitely remain within those limits. Imagine a clear blue rug lying in a room where the main colors were pinks (red group) and apricots and gold-beige (yellow group). Not only would the blue destroy the harmony of the color balance of the room but the beauty of the rug itself would be lost. Using all three primary colors is better left to experts, and even they may need a little luck to produce a successful combination. However, there is no reason why you should not use the full scale of shades of the colors you are working with.

Now, instead of a clear blue rug, imagine a deep ruby-colored Afghan in our pink and gold-beige room. The Afghan rug would supply a touch of drama and help to highlight the pastel colors in the room. A modern "silk-washed" black Chinese rug with the design woven in pinks and golds would suit a traditional room so long as the room is a big one. So would an antique Aubusson or Savonnerie with a brownish-black background and the designs picked out in creams, pinks and golds. (There is only one drawback to this particular scheme: these types of antique rugs are rare and among the most expensive pieces you can buy.)

If you live in a hot climate and find that the idea of a pink and gold-beige room is too warm, try adding a large area of pale stone or oatmeal colors to it. These neutral tones have a remarkably cooling effect. The natural undyed colors of the Persian Verdose pieces might be suitable. Or try using a Berber rug; these also are usually made in the natural colors of the wool.

An oriental rug can help unite a room that has too many colors. Choose a rug that contains each of the colors, then change your walls or draperies to match the predominant color of the rug. Complete the effect by accentuating the major color with lamps, cushions and ornaments. Chances are that if you use the rug as a color guide, the room will come together.

You can complement the mood of your room with even a single small rug. A client of mine wanted an investment piece that she could eventually sell to put her son through college. She didn't plan to walk on the rug so we were free to choose a silk one. The sitting room in which the rug was to live was decorated in pastel shades of turquoise with touches of coral. We found a silk Turkish prayer rug of a shimmering russet color. Draped over a chest, the rug added a touch of pure glamour to the room—so much so that now my client wonders how she will be able to part with the rug when the time comes.

DESIGNING A ROOM FOR YOUR RUG

If you ever have the opportunity to decorate starting from scratch, try taking your entire scheme from a rug. Obviously, the proportions of the rug should suit the room you have in mind and the price of the rug should suit your pocket. But aside from these practical considerations, try simply window shopping for rugs that please you and that you feel suit your personality.

Make a note of each rug that you like with a short description of its colors. Write down whether the design is curvilinear or rectilinear. After you have looked at many rugs, study your list. Perhaps all the rugs you have noted are pastel; or perhaps they are all geometric; or maybe they all contain a particular color combination. If you have noted enough rugs, then you should definitely be able to see your personal preferences emerging.

Next, decide which two or three rugs are your favorites. Then, using the color schemes of these rugs, imagine your room decorated to match. Do this for each of your favorite rugs, making notes as you go along. Unless you are feeling very confident, it is a good idea to wait a day or two before making a final decision on which rug you want. It is especially important to analyze the color structure of your rug in relation to the colors you would like for your room. Remember that a color appears to change when seen next to a contrasting color or due to its mass. This is particularly true of yellow.

I once decorated a room using a Persian Kirman rug as my guide. The Kirman had a soft golden yellow central medallion on a creamy white field. The border repeated the medallion design with the same soft yellow and with light and dark blues. I painted the room in what I thought was going to be a very soft

A Saruk rug, circa *1930.*

buttercup yellow. When I stood back to admire my handiwork, I saw that, due to its mass, the yellow was so intense that I had no alternative but to start over. My Kirman merely looked faded in the room. I diluted the yellow paint four-to-one with white paint, so that it looked creamy on the brush. When I had finished the room for the second time, the yellow was still far too bright. Rather than paint the room a third time, I counterbalanced the yellow with cornflower blue and white draperies and painted the cornices and the door and window frames white. The final result was quite pretty, but I always had the feeling that my Persian Kirman would have looked better with the soft color I had in mind in the first place.

DEFINING AREAS WITH RUGS

Oriental rugs can help to divide a very large room visually. For example, if you have one room that has separate living, dining and study areas you could use three orientals with different background colors to set off each area. For your living area you might choose a cream-ground Persian Kashan rug that has blues and golds in its curvilinear design. Then you could place a Persian Saruk in your dining area. These rugs are known for their coral background. The Saruk also has a curvilinear design and would include touches of the blues and golds of the Kashan. For the study area, you could use blue as a background, perhaps choosing a fine Isfahan with the curving Shah Abbas design and its subtly colored creamy beiges.

There are hundreds of combinations of rugs to choose from depending on your preference and the style of your home. Whichever combination you use, the visual separation of the rugs should be highlighted by wide aisles of polished wood or tile floors or of plain, light-toned wall-to-wall carpeting. A neutral beige works well for almost any color combination of rugs. An independent lighting group for each area would complete the effect of visual separation.

Oriental rugs can also be used to "furnish" an area of your home that seems rather bare, for example, a corridor or a small foyer. The rug, together with a mirror to reflect it, is often all the decoration the area needs.

HANGING YOUR RUG

In addition to defining a room visually by using different rugs on the floor, you can hang oriental rugs as room dividers to define areas. Only very thin rugs should be used in this way; in fact, the thinner they are, the more effective they will look.

To hang a rug, sandwich the edge of the rug between two three-inch (8 cm.) strips of wood or lucite, leaving one and one-half inches (4.5 cm.) at the edges. Use a small clamp at either end of the strips to lock them tightly together and bore a small hole into the ends. Next, securely fasten two hooks into the ceiling. Thread colorless heavy-duty fishing line through the holes in the strips and suspend the rug from the ceiling hooks so that the bottom edge is about six inches (15 cm.) off the floor.

If you want to hang your rug against the wall like a painting there are two methods that can be used. I prefer the first method below and have found it to be the safest and most practicable.

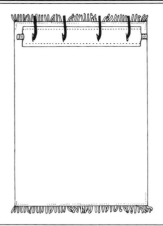

A tube of webbing is sewn to the back of the rug. Then a brass rod is inserted through the tube and suspended from four hooks on the wall.

Using three-inch-wide (8 cm.) webbing, hand-sew a tube to the back of the rug, one half-inch (1.5 cm.) from and parallel to the edge from which the rug will hang. Stitch through the rug and the webbing with large tacking stitches on the back and small tacking stitches on the face of the rug. The stitches on the front will disappear into the pile. Next, have a brass rod cut to measure one half-inch (1.5 cm.) less than the length of the webbing tube and insert the rod into the tube. Line up three or four hooks on the wall where the rug will hang. Then, with a razor blade, nick the webbing in places to line up with the hooks on the wall. Through the cuts in the webbing, the rod can be hung from the hooks. Your rug will hang neatly in place and can easily be taken down when it needs to be brushed (see Chapter 6).

The second method is not recommended for fine pieces. For this method, nail a piece of "gripper board" directly onto the wall. Then simply press your rug onto the spokes of the gripper board. Be sure the board is securely fastened or the weight of the rug may pull it loose from the wall. Surprisingly, this method doesn't seem to damage rugs; but, again, I do not recommend it for very fine pieces. I also advise against the old-fashioned method of sewing curtain rings onto the back of the rug and threading a rod through them. The weight of the rug tends to pull it out of shape if it is left this way for any length of time.

Oriental rugs can be very effective when they are hung in place of paintings. The rich colors and intricate designs are even more beautiful and noticeable when the rugs are hanging than when you are walking over them. A big rug hung on the wall will have all the impact and drama of a large painting, besides being a more unusual decoration.

If your home has a staircase, try hanging a rug on the half-landing where it will be seen as people go upstairs. Or if you have a fireplace, try placing small three-by-two-foot (.91 × .61 m.) Pushti-size rugs on either side of it, hanging them just below the level of the mantelshelf. Alternatively, a long thin Saph rug, about five by two feet, six inches (1.52 × .76 m.), with the family prayer-rug design running horizontally across it could be hung parallel to the mantelshelf. This same type of rug can also look magnificent when it is hung on the wall behind a long buffet, especially when the rug is hung no more than a few inches above the buffet.

An additional benefit from hanging rugs on walls is that they absorb sound as effectively as baffle boards. You might keep this in mind, whether you want to prevent a large room from echoing or keep the neighbors from complaining about your stereo system.

SENSITIVITY TO LIGHT

Pakistan rugs are particularly sensitive to light. By this I do not mean that they fade or that their colors are unfast. I mean that light produces "instant changes" as it reflects off the glossy wool. Depending on which way the pile of the rug is facing or which way light is falling on it, rose can appear to change to red, or a pale gold may suddenly look brown. The phenomenon is even more pronounced in silk pieces, wherever they were made. If you are thinking of buying a Pakistan piece, it is particularly important to look at it from all angles. And if you are planning to hang the rug on a wall, be sure to ask the salesperson to hold it up so that you can see exactly what the effect is going to be.

This reaction to light can be used to highlight any of your rugs whether they are on the wall or on the floor. Directing a spotlight onto the rug will produce a glowing effect which works especially well if the rug is wool inlaid with silk. The part of the design that has been woven in silk will shine more brightly than the woolen parts of the rug, which will have a softer gleam.

ODDS AND ENDS

Don't throw out a rug that has been damaged beyond repair. The best parts can be used to cover benches or stools or pillows or be used as a tiny mat underneath the telephone. These miniature "orientals" also make attractive table mats. Just bind the edges with a matching wool using a blanket stitch and add a length of store-bought fringe to either end. To give an antique flavor to your room, make a Victorian antimacassar by placing a mat over the back of an upholstered chair. There are dozens of ways to use these little rugs. You might even make a set for your car!

A small rug or a pretty piece of one can make an unusual tabletop. Find or build a table with a top that is an inch or two smaller than the size of your rug. Pin the edges of the rug to the sides of the table with picture nails. Or, if it is a thin rug, you can use a staple gun. Then have a sheet of glass cut to cover the tabletop. To neaten the edges of the glass, you can use lengths of picture frame, mitered at the corners. If you prefer a softer frame, glue three-inch-wide (8 cm.) upholstery braid around the edges.

For truly unique decorations you might try to find woven saddlebags and grain sacks. These make unusually attractive and durable floor cushions. They are already sewn together on three sides, so just fill them with a pillow or pillow-stuffing and close the remaining side. Use strong button thread and large tacking stitches.

Also worth hunting for are the one-foot-square saddlebags, called *torbas*, made to be worn by goats; the *dis-torbas* that the nomadic tribespeople use as shoulder bags; and the small *ghashoghdoun*, which is part of the nomad's version of our chest of drawers. Hung on the inside of the tent, various bags hold clothing, brushes, jewelry and other personal possessions. The small hammock-shaped bags, *tobrehs*, are meant for hanging over the entrance to the tent so that people can place their shoes in them as they enter. This serves to keep the floor of the tent clear—and also makes it less likely that a scorpion will be sitting inside a shoe when the owner comes to put it on again.

These bags make unusual wall decorations. Hang two or three on a wall in your kitchen and fill them with wooden spoons, shiny copper cooking implements or leafy sprays of herbs. Or hang one in your bathroom to hold your own brushes and combs. Obviously, there are dozens of ways to use them.

DECORATING WITH KELIMS

The versatile, flat-woven kelim pieces can be hung on walls and windows or draped over tables, chairs and chests. An especially interesting way to use a very large kelim is to hang it from the ceiling to create a tentlike effect. You might try it in your dining area, or perhaps over your bed. Be sure to use the largest and most flexible kelim you can find. Use a staple gun to fasten each of the four corners of the kelim to the ceiling. Leave plenty of slack so that the center of the kelim billows downward. After you have stapled the corners, put a staple through the center point of the kelim to fasten it to the ceiling. This treatment should not damage your rug so long as you remove the staples carefully when you want to take it down. The tent effect can be further emphasized by stapling additional kelims to the walls. Try to choose pieces that match one another in tone. It is unnecessary to match the designs, but the scale of the designs should be similar.

I once used this scheme in a very small dining area that had no windows. My client had a circular glass dining table over which we suspended a crystal chandelier, with the chain running up to the center point of a kelim on the ceiling. This kelim was woven with return weft threads (as most of them are) which leave a gap every four or five inches (10 or 13 cm.). We were able to thread the chain and electrical cord through the kelim and to connect it to the electrical ceiling fixture. The contrasts produced by the kelim, the glass table and the crystal chandelier were startling. The drab, uninviting area became an attractive small room.

"Curtain" kelims can be used as false draperies in window treatment schemes. They will often have been woven to use as curtains for the entrance to the tents of nomadic tribes. They are made in strips approximately two and a half feet wide by seven or eight feet long (.76 × 2.13 or 2.44 m.). Curtain kelims are not rare and you should be able to find such pieces in rug stores. If they are sewn together with a tacking stitch when you get them, you can easily see the central seam and can unpick it.

In a contemporary setting, try using geometric kelim strips hung flat to the wall on either side of a window that has a vertical blind. Staple a third strip across the top of the window, like a flat valance. Make sure that the ends of the valance line up with the outermost edges of the vertical strips. This window treatment gives a tailored look without being unduly severe. It will also help to keep out drafts.

Another way to use kelims is as covers for divans or chests. This also looks especially nice in contemporary settings where the kelims make a lively contrast to stark modern furniture. And, as I mentioned earlier, kelims are usually made of cotton and colorfast ones (remember the handkerchief test) are easily laundered.

The Indian version of kelims, the dhurris, are becoming very popular in Europe and America because of their wide variety of

Left to right: Azerbaijan, Shiraz and Kurdish kelim designs.

designs and colors and their relatively low prices. The standard size for dhurris is six feet, nine inches by three feet, eight inches (2.06 × 1.12 m.). This is the size of the Indian string beds, called *charpoys*. Indian dhurris woven in this size normally cost between $120 and $180 in the retail market. The Persian, Turkish and Afghan kelims can be found for $800 to $1200 in the retail stores. The reason that kelims cost so much more than dhurris is that kelims usually are larger, with more intricate designs. A single kelim may take two or three months to weave, whereas a dhurri weaver can produce three charpoy-sized rugs in a day.

The classical antique dhurris have a pliant texture and soft timeworn colors. They may be difficult to find and will cost hundreds of dollars. I recently heard of a piece being sold for $6,500 (which makes little sense when you compare it with investment-quality Persian or Turkish rugs). However, the inexpensive dhurris are definitely worth looking for as an attractive alternative to the more expensive pile rugs.

Weaver working at an upright loom, knotting an almost completed Isfahan rug.

Vacation - A time to rest, relax, have fun & explore...

Explore the Basics of Photography this Summer in the Sun!

If you have a 35mm manual camera and would like to understand a little more about your camera and photography, Susanne M. Champa, local photographer, would be happy to share her knowledge with you.

Discover your camera... Develop your creativity.

Days: Weds.: 3:00-5:00PM
Thurs. & Fri.: 9:00-11:00AM
Location: On the beautiful seaside grounds of the Ralph Waldo Emerson Inn. We will meet in the main lobby at 2:55PM & 8:55AM.
Fee: $25 per 2-hour session.
To Register & For More Information: Call Susanne M. Champa at 546-8048.

CHAPTER SIX

First Aid

Once you have become the proud owner of an oriental rug, it is important that you know how to look after it. In general, these rugs are very strong. Because each tuft is individually knotted around the foundation warp and weft threads, unlike a machine-made rug where the tufts are simply looped around the foundation threads, your oriental is almost indestructible. Given a minimal amount of care, it should last through many generations to become a cherished family heirloom.

PADDING

No matter how smooth your floor may be, always place some form of padding (cut ¾ of an inch [2.3 cm.] smaller than the rug) between the floor and your oriental rug. This has three advantages: the unprotected underside of your rug won't wear out; the rug will be much softer to walk on; and it won't slip from beneath your feet as you hurry to answer the telephone.

If you plan to put the rug on a polished floor you will need one of the synthetic rubber underlays sold by stores that sell wall-to-wall carpeting. A thin layer of underfelt combined with the springy underlay will provide insulation and help discourage moths. If you have a rug on the lean side (½ inch [1.5 cm.] or less thick), choose an underlay with a shiny smooth topside so that the oriental can lie smoothly on top and the slip-resistant underside of the padding can grip the floor. A word of caution: Don't use the sheets of plain foam rubber on a polished floor. Foam rubber tends to collect moisture that will eventually soften the polish on the floor, and you will end up with a sticky mess. The damp will also rot your rug.

An annoying problem that often affects expensive, finely woven rugs is that their edges tend to curl under. This problem is easily dealt with: just slightly damp the offending edge and roll up the rug diagonally, smoothing out the curl as you do so. Leave it to set overnight, propped against a chair leg to prevent its unrolling. When you are sure the rug is dry, unroll it and the rug will lie perfectly flat. You may need to repeat this process from time to time. Alternatively, you can take the rug to a professional repairer who will uncurl the edges by inserting a stitch every few inches. *Never* attempt to uncurl the rug yourself by snipping threads to relax the curl.

If you plan to place your oriental rug on top of wall-to-wall carpeting, the carpeting should have a short pile. Shag carpeting and oriental rugs never mix. A good buy is the low-pile commercial wall-to-wall carpeting that banks and department stores have found to be so serviceable. If the pile of your carpet is deep, the oriental rug will wrinkle easily and "float" about. However, there are ways around this problem. Try sandwiching a rough towel between the rug and the carpeting. The towel will grip both the carpeting and the rug so that the rug will stay flat. (Newspapers may also work, but if your carpeting is a light color this is not advisable because the newsprint could mark it.) The nicest solution is to use a product called Rugstop, available through oriental rug dealers. This looks like flat sheets of cotton candy and is so lightweight that I can lift a twenty-five-yard (22.85 m.) roll with one hand. Rugstop grips both the underside of the oriental and the topside of the carpeting, holding the rug firmly in place. (See page 242 for name of supplier.)

Once your rug is padded correctly and assuming that it is a relatively modern one and free from wear, you have little else to worry about. If it is properly padded, even heavy wooden furniture should not damage it, so long as the base of the furniture is not sharp and no friction occurs.

WEAR AND TEAR

I was recently asked to value a Persian Heriz rug, on the center of which was standing a solid oak refectory dining table capable of seating fourteen people. When the table was moved so that

A woolen Heriz rug can be a good choice for a dining room. Heriz are made in large sizes, are relatively sturdy, are inexpensive, and often have a sufficiently detailed design to mask accidental spills.

I could examine the rug, I saw six half-inch (1.5 cm.)-deep indentations that had been made by the legs of the table, the bottoms of which were smooth and broad. My client was most upset, thinking the rug was spoiled. She told me that the dining room had been arranged six years earlier when the family had moved into the house and because the table was so heavy it had not been moved since. After I finished evaluating the rug, we rearranged the table so that the legs were no longer resting on the same spots. I then took a damp nailbrush and brushed against the flattened pile, finishing by brushing in the direction of the pile. A week later my client telephoned me to say that the dents were gone and the rug looked as good as new. Luckily, the legs of that table were wooden. If the feet of your furniture are sharp, or if they are made of metal or if they have small casters attached to them, you must use protectors before putting this type of furniture on top of your rug.

In the example I just gave, if the nailbrush method had not removed the indentations, I would have recommended that they be steamed. To steam a dent in your rug, first place a rough terry-cloth towel over the dent. Then, pressing very lightly, steam over that area with your steam iron set on "wool." The towel is very important: it protects the rug from scorching and the pile of the towel leaves space for the pile of the rug to rise. After steaming, allow the rug to dry thoroughly. If necessary, repeat the process every two or three days until the mark is gone.

You may also steam silk rugs to remove creases, although the process is slightly different. Lay the rug face up on a clean and completely smooth surface. Place a damp (*not* wet) cloth on top of the crease and, using quick light strokes in the direction of the pile, iron it with a *cool* iron (the setting marked "silk"). Do not rest the iron on the cloth—do not even pause for an instant in your ironing motion—or the outline of the iron may appear on the surface of the rug. If the crease does not come out at first, repeat the process every two days or so. Remember to allow the rug to air-dry thoroughly away from direct heat after each steaming.

If you are nervous about pressing the face of the rug, then steam it from the reverse side, following the directions given above. Continual dampness is a great enemy of oriental rugs and can cause serious damage, so after any treatment be certain that the rug dries completely. Dry the front *first* and then the back; very little air reaches the underside of a rug that is lying on the floor so, even if the pile appears to be dry, the back of the rug may become soggy and silently disintegrate.

Obviously, no matter how strongly a textile is made, the more wear and tear it receives, the faster it will wear out. Oriental rugs are no exception to this rule. This is why I always recommend that rugs be regularly reversed (turned from end to end, not upside down) or moved a few inches in any direction. Ideally this should be done every six months, although once a year will help. Moving rugs about in this way alters the tread pattern and helps to prevent low patches from appearing after a few years of use. If you have more than one rug, try swapping them around. For instance, the one in the bedroom could be placed in the hallway or living room and vice versa. If you move your rugs around, they will last almost indefinitely. Besides, most rugs are versatile and, as you help to preserve them, they can give your decor an interesting new look.

FADING

Clients often ask if rugs fade, and of course they do. Any light will gradually mellow color. A client once brought me a Turkish Kayseri prayer rug that she and her husband had bought when they were living in Turkey a few years earlier. Originally, the rug's predominant color was a deep sapphire blue which perfectly matched their collection of Chinese porcelain. The problem was that, by the time I saw it, the color had changed to a faded turquoise. They wanted to know if anything could be done to restore the rug to its original color. I explained that although the rug could be tinted, there was no guarantee as to how pleasing or how permanent the effect would be.

The drastic change of color puzzled me. Light will gradually soften colors; but going from dark sapphire to pale turquoise in a few years was very unusual. My client then explained that the living room of their house in Turkey had a floor-to-ceiling picture window that directly overlooked the sea. The rug had been placed in front of the window and the combination of strong Turkish sunshine and light reflected off the water had virtually bleached it. Fortunately, the rug had been evenly exposed to the light so that at least it had not become patchy.

In northern climates the change in color from fading is almost imperceptible, although if one part of your rug is always in shadow while the rest of the rug is exposed to daylight, you may find that eventually the coloring will become unbalanced. If you put your rug close to a window, turn it frequently so that all parts of it receive an equal amount of light. Sheer curtains are helpful in taking the edge off very bright light; if your windows have these it is unlikely that you will notice any change in the color of your rug for many years.

Light seldom has a disagreeable effect on correctly dyed rugs. Usually it serves only to mellow and harmonize their colors, which is one of the appealing aspects of the older pieces. The exceptions are the aniline-dyed rugs discussed in Chapter 3. If you happen to own one of these rugs, it should be kept in the darkest area of your home (preferably a closet). Better still, auction it!

Sometimes the fact that light mellows color can be an advantage. One of the first rugs that I bought was a Persian silk Qum with a forest design made up of small flowering trees with birds fluttering among the branches. When I took it home, I realized that the vibrant scarlet in the rug overpowered everything else in the room. Finally I decided to hang the rug out of the way on the wall of a staircase where it was lit by a northern window. Four years later when I was moving to another house, the rug was taken down. I found that although all the other colors appeared to be unchanged, the scarlet silk was no longer vivid. The light had softened it to a muted ruby color with a golden sheen. I kept the rug for years in my new home and for a while I had it in front of a southern window. But the colors never again appeared to change. The Qum just lay there, looking beautiful. (I was finally persuaded to sell it to the owner of an appropriately grand French chateau where, as far as I know, it remains today.)

REGULAR CLEANING

People often wonder whether or not they should vacuum their oriental rugs. The answer is, yes, vacuuming your rug once a week is a fast and efficient way to remove the grit that might cut into the foundation threads. However, for *weekly* vacuuming use a vacuum that works only on suction and does *not* beat the rug. Always stroke the rug in the direction of the pile or from side to side; vacuuming against the pile leaves it raised and allows grit to reach the knots more quickly. Always avoid vacuuming the delicate fringe area—your rug could end up in the bag. For daily cleansing a small carpet sweeper is ideal.

Once (ideally, twice) a year the beating type of vacuum should be used on both the front and back of the rug to help remove any buildup of grit. This applies to wool rugs only. Silk rugs are less robust so *never* use a vacuum cleaner on them. Harsh treatment in any form can do untold damage to them. I recommend weekly brushing with a medium-soft nylon or bristle—never wire—brush and a thorough, but gentle, shaking once a month. The woolen silk-inlaid rugs can be vacuumed like the pure woolen ones, but don't press hard on the silk bits. To take care of kelims (or any rugs, for that matter) that you hang on walls, simply brush them lightly, also with a medium-soft brush, once or twice a month.

A sneaky enemy of your rug is moths. There are many moth-proofing sprays available but be *sure* to read the directions and the precautions before using them on your precious rug. An old-fashioned but safe way to avoid moths breakfasting off your rug is to create a diversion: hide several open dishes of feathers about the room, on the tops of tall cupboards and bookcases. Moths love feathers more than anything else so, ignoring your rug, they will lay their eggs in the feathers. By checking your traps every so often you can get rid of the moths before they become a problem.

The most moth-prone part of your rug is any part that is tucked under furniture. Moths like these quiet dark places, so regular cleaning really is necessary to avoid damage. Heat also kills moths, so putting your rug in the hot sun for a few hours every now and then is a good precaution. Once or twice a year, when you have finished vacuuming the underside of your rug, take the additional precaution against moths of lightly dusting the back of your rug with camphor powder. Moths are most active in June, July and August, so concentrate your moth-proofing campaign in these months. Don't forget the rugs hanging on the wall—moths crawl in behind them to lay their eggs. A light dusting of camphor powder on the back of the rug and a vigorous, but gentle, shaking once a week throughout the summer months should do the trick.

Oriental rugs tend to "wear" clean so that, aside from dealing with the occasional stain, regular brushing or vacuuming is all that is necessary to keep them clean. Having your rug cleaned too frequently may damage the fibers, so if the rug was clean when you bought it, you should only have to cope with a major cleaning once every five to seven years.

MAJOR CLEANING

When you decide that your rug does need a major cleaning, the first step is to do the handkerchief test mentioned in Chapter 3. Spit on a corner of a white handkerchief (saliva is alkaline) and rub the background color of the rug. Then examine the hand-kerchief to see if any of the dye has stained it. If the handkerchief remains white, repeat the test on each of the other colors in the rug. If the handkerchief becomes deeply stained from any of the colors, you have a serious problem. Wetting the rug could cause the colors to bleed into each other. Many vegetable dyes are to some degree not colorfast, although they may only slightly stain the handkerchief.

If your rug fails the handkerchief test, do *not* try to work on it yourself. Instead, go to your nearest oriental rug store and ask them to arrange to have the rug cleaned for you. It is important to tell them that the colors may be unfast. If the store is unhelpful or too far away, try telephoning one of the better-known auction houses. They will often recommend specialist oriental rug cleaners in your area. Alternatively, you can seek advice from the National Institute of Rug Cleaners, a division of AIDS International (2009 North 14th Street, Arlington, Va. 22201; 703-524-8120). Never give your rug to a regular dry cleaner. The chemicals they may use could destroy the natural fats in the wool, the wool itself, the patina or the coloring.

After you have done the handkerchief test and you are certain that each of the colors in the rug is fast, there are two other points to consider: Rugs take a long time to dry and while they are wet they smell rather like a wet dog! So when washing your rug at home, try to do it in the summertime so you can do it outdoors. Rugs are very heavy when they are wet so wash them in the garden where you will have a garden hose to rinse them off and plenty of space to spread them flat while you are washing and drying them. If you dry your rug on the lawn, do it just before the grass is cut. The longer grass will help air to circulate under the rug. Professional rug cleaners use a flat slatted base raised a few inches off the ground. No matter how sound the dyes may be in your rug, they can still bleed if the wet rug is not kept flat in freely circulating air.

To wash a woolen rug, use a baby shampoo, pure soap flakes or diluted liquid Woolite. A shampoo called Saponaria (at the moment available only in Europe) is especially suitable for woolen oriental rugs, or use Novel Treat Carpet Shampoo, which has the added advantage of not making it necessary to wet the rug unduly. To use Novel Treat, simply dilute it as directed and sponge it on. When it has dried to crystals, vacuum thoroughly. Never use detergents or commercial carpet shampoos. These products often contain bleach which could damage the wool of an oriental rug.

Never attempt to shampoo a rug made from silk. The soap could "explode" the tips of the fibers so that they spread, making them look cloudy and fuzzy. Instead, dilute white vinegar in cool water (one part vinegar to three parts water). Spread the rug out flat. Next, take a soft clean chamois cloth (be sure it is real chamois leather and not a synthetic), dip it into the vinegar-water and squeeze it out hard. Keeping it flat, gently rub the surface of the rug in the direction of the pile. Air-dry the rug away from direct heat until it is perfectly dry. Finish by polishing the rug with a clean dry chamois in the direction of the pile.

The Scandinavians have an interesting method for cleaning their rugs. After a heavy fall of snow, they put the rug in the garage overnight so that it gets very cold. In the morning the cold rug (a warm rug would melt the snow and become soggy) is laid face down on the fresh snow and gently beaten with twigs to loosen the dirt. The rug is left to "settle" for fifteen minutes lying on its face, then it is picked up and shaken energetically. The now sparkling rug is carried back indoors and spread out flat to dry. This is a good way to clean rugs—so long as you have nice clean, powdery snow.

Whichever way you choose to clean your rug, always remember to air-dry it thoroughly, away from any artificial heat. When the face of the rug is completely dry, turn the rug over until the underside is also completely dry; otherwise mildew could set in, causing your rug to rot.

MENDING

The old saying "A stitch in time saves nine" is especially true for oriental rugs. Early attention to a damaged area will not only save you hundreds of "stitches" but hundreds of dollars as well. To check for potential weak spots in your rug, try holding it up to the light. This is particularly important for older rugs. If there are weak areas, sewing a felt pad to cover the entire back of the rug will help protect them. Next, run your hand over the surface of the rug to see if you can find any low spots where the pile has been worn away. If there are low spots, try to position the rug so that the family avoids constantly stepping on them. The side cords and fringes are especially sensitive.

If the damaged area is a hole, transparent Scotch tape can be used to prevent it from getting worse before you have time to mend it. Turn the rug on its face and stick the tape on the back of the hole, making sure that all the edges are covered. Press the tape down firmly, warming it with your hand until you are sure it has stuck. Taking care not to crease the tape, turn the rug right side up. From the front, press down any loose threads onto the tape. If the tape doesn't stick, it is probably too cold. Try placing a piece of brown paper over the taped hole, warming a heavy flat-bottomed dish in the oven and then standing the dish on the brown paper for a moment or two. *Never* use a liquid rubber solution to repair a rug. If you do, it will be impossible later to have the rug professionally mended because the rubber jams the fibers together. Also, never use glue or any tape other than the transparent kind. Countless numbers of rugs have been ruined because of these amateur repairs.

Darning is a good way to mend medium or small holes in inexpensive rugs. But don't cut away any of the loose threads of the rug—just fold them back out of sight. If your rug is an old one, "weather" your darning wool to age the colors so that they will blend more naturally with the old wools of the rug. You can do this by exposing the new wool to the sun for a few days.

If a hole is too large to darn, try patching it with a piece cut from a discarded rug. Fragments of oriental rugs can sometimes be bought at small auction sales, or your local dealer may sell you a suitable piece. Cut the patch to size and sew it into position. Matching up *lines* in the pattern is more important than matching up small designs. The eye immediately notices a break in a straight line, but it will often miss the fact that a section of small flowers, for example, has a patch of small diamonds in the middle of it. When you are sewing the piece in place, make sure that the pile of the patch and the pile of the rug are facing in the same direction. When you have finished sewing, brush around the edges of the patch so that it blends into the rug.

Valuable rugs should always be taken to a professional repairer, who will often be able to "invisibly" mend them. If the problem is a hole, this will most likely involve a reweave. Reweaving is a highly skilled and time-consuming process so it is bound to be expensive. However, if the repairer is good and does the job properly, it will be worth the money to have your rug rewoven. Ask to look at examples of the repairer's work. If it is good, you should not be able to see the stitches at all on the front and you should hardly be able to see them on the back. Because reweaving is so expensive, always settle the price before the work begins.

If your local oriental rug dealer prefers not to handle repairs, write to the curator of an appropriate museum; he may be able to recommend someone. Another way to find a good repairer is to ask a specialist oriental-rug cleaning company; they might have a repairer on their staff. Or, again, you could contact the National Institute of Rug Cleaners (703-524-8120). Your local auctioneer might also be able to recommend someone. Or ask the buyer for the oriental rug department of a large store to suggest a repairer.

However, because professional repairs cost so much, I recommend that you try doing the job yourself unless the rug is a valuable one. As long as you don't use scissors, you won't harm the rug. If the job turns out to be too much for you, you can always call in a professional.

PROTECTING THE FRINGES

The fringes are the most vulnerable part of an oriental rug and if they unravel, the whole rug could eventually unravel. You may notice that the end borders of some antique rugs are missing; this is usually because their fringes were loose and not "stopped" in time. So check the fringes carefully. If they are unraveling, you can stop them by using button thread and a blanket stitch to hold the weft threads in place.

Ordinary clear Scotch tape can also be helpful if a fringe needs first aid and you have no time to do the repair. I once stuck it onto the back of a rug of my own as a temporary way to "stop" its fringe. I forgot all about the tape until six months later when I noticed it as I was spring cleaning. The tape had held perfectly and the fringe was no worse than it had been.

Never, never cut a fringe off. When my mother was seventeen she inherited a collection of oriental rugs from her guardian. One of these had a six-inch-long (15 cm.) silk fringe which Mother thought looked untidy. Instead of folding the fringe back underneath the rug and sticking it in place with tape, Mother took a pair of scissors and cut the whole fringe off. Over the years the rug unraveled and we ended up using it to line the dog's basket. Sadly, I now know that the rug was an extremely rare circular silk Tabriz. For sentimental reasons I have sent it back to Persia to be rewoven; when the work is done the rug may be worth $4,000 or slightly more. If Mother had known how to keep the rug in good condition, its realistic auction value today would be over $50,000.

So if you feel that the fringe of your rug is too long and looks untidy, try knotting it: gather a few strands together and tie a single loose knot. Do not tighten the knot until you have finished knotting the whole length of the fringe. Then tighten the knots, lining them up as you go so that they form a straight line. Knotting a fringe is time-consuming, but it will make the rug look neater and help prevent the fringe from unraveling.

I once spent an entire evening knotting a fringe while my small Shetland sheep dog kept me company. When I spread the rug on the floor and stood back to admire my handiwork, she walked over to it and deliberately bit through one of the tassels. I mended this with Scotch tape. I still haven't gotten around to sewing the tassel back on and almost a year later, the rug is still lying there and the tape is holding well.

One other place to check for damage is the selvage cord of your rug. These side cords, the *candys*, run along the two outside edges of a rug. If they are becoming detached from the rug, sew them back in place with button thread and blanket stitches. If the candys are missing and the sides are beginning to fray, you can make your own candys. Take a length of string and wrap it with wool that matches the color of the border of your rug. Then sew this cord into place with button thread and your rug will be as good as new.

TINTING

If your fringe problem is that it is too white, you can tone it down. All you need is a pot of strong coffee (the instant kind is fine) and a pot of strongly brewed tea made from four or five tea bags. Spread the rug out flat and generously sponge its fringes, using the tea first. Try to work your way quickly along the full length of the fringe so that you avoid forming "high-tide" marks. The color may seem rather dark but it will lighten considerably as the cotton dries. Later, you can adjust the color by repeating the process, this time using the coffee. Provided your rug has successfully passed the handkerchief test, you won't have to worry too much if a little of the coffee or tea spreads onto the wool. Just rub the wool immediately with plain water and then rub it dry again with a clean cloth, finishing by rubbing in the direction of the pile.

Other areas of a rug besides the fringe can be tinted as well. Suppose you found an old worn-out rug which your dealer assured you was not a valuable piece. Nevertheless, after you shampooed it, the rug looked quite pretty—except for a couple of bald patches. To restore the rug, buy yourself some waterproof felt-tipped pens, choosing as varied a selection of colors as you can find. Match up the pen colors with the colors in the rug and ink in the missing pattern. If the design is missing too, try tracing a corresponding part of the design onto the bare spot. This idea sounds crude but it is frequently practiced by many professionals, and it works.

STAINS

Accidents do happen, so keep a large bottle of plain soda water readily available. If a glass of red or white wine spills on your rug, pour soda water on it immediately. This will dilute the wine and the bubbles will help to lift the stain out as you blot it lightly with an absorbent dry cloth or paper towel. Soda water works well on most stains and most fabrics too, if you are able to use it quickly enough. Be sure to use only *plain* soda water, rather than any of the flavored types, or you could end up with a worse mess than you started with.

Stains that have been allowed to dry are much more difficult to deal with, although dried mud and even blood can often be simply brushed away. So work on the stain as soon as possible. I am not making any promises nor giving any guarantees, but here is a list of remedies that have worked for me over the years. Before trying any of them, remember these points:

1. Quickly blot up or scrape up as much of the mess as you can, taking care not to rub it into the pile (except chewing gum, which should be cooled first; see chart).
2. Keep the rug flat at all times.
3. *Before* using a remedy, test it on a small, inconspicuous part of your rug. *Always do the handkerchief test first.*
4. *Never* use soap or shampoo on a silk rug. Use the vinegar-water/ chamois-cloth method instead. Any stain on a silk rug that does not respond to this method should be left alone and professional help should be sought as soon as possible. The National Institute of Rug Cleaners should be able to advise you on where to take your rug. Their telephone number is 703-524-8120.
5. Never use a shampoo that contains any bleach. Use Novel Treat Carpet Shampoo or any similar crystallizing shampoo that your rug dealer assures you is safe.

Stain	Remedy
Whiskey (alcohol)	Try plain soda water first. Blot stain with white blotting paper or paper towel. Then wipe stain with clean white cloth moistened with methylated spirits (the colorless industrial kind is best). Wipe in direction of pile. Air-dry thoroughly away from direct heat. If that doesn't work, make solution of crystallizing shampoo or baby shampoo. Add 1 teaspoon white vinegar per pint. If using baby shampoo, rinse well with clear water. While damp, brush in direction of pile with medium-soft bristle or nylon brush. Air-dry away from direct heat.
Food generally and all dairy products except butter	Wipe gently with clean white cloth moistened with solvent such as white spirit or carbon tetrachloride. If using carbon tetrachloride, *always use a face mask* to avoid breathing the fumes. Make solution of crystallizing shampoo or baby shampoo. Add 1 teaspoon white vinegar per pint. If using baby shampoo, rinse well with clear water. Using medium-soft nylon or bristle brush, brush in direction of pile. Air-dry thoroughly away from direct heat. If stain remains when rug is dry, dampen it again with warm water and cover with mixture of 1 teaspoon of photographer's hypo-

Stain	Remedy
	crystals (ask your pharmacist) in generous cup of water. Keep stain moist at least two hours by covering with damp cloth. Rinse well with clear water. Brush with medium-soft nylon or bristle brush in direction of pile. Air-dry away from direct heat.
Grease stains such as butter, or sticky stains such as tar or paint	Rub with white spirit or carbon tetrachloride— *remember to wear a face mask.* While still moist, make solution of crystallizing shampoo or baby shampoo. Add 1 teaspoon white vinegar per pint; wash stain. If using baby shampoo, rinse with clear water. Brush with medium-soft bristle or nylon brush in direction of pile. Air-dry thoroughly away from direct heat.
Animal	As fast as you can (uric acid bleaches color and destroys wool), flush stain three or four times with plain soda water, blotting with white paper towel each time. Make solution of crystallizing shampoo or baby shampoo. Add 1 teaspoon white vinegar per pint. If using baby shampoo, rinse well with clear water. Brush in direction of pile with medium-soft nylon or bristle brush. Air-dry thoroughly away from direct heat.
Dried blood	First try brushing stain with stiff brush (nylon or bristle, not wire). If the stain persists, dampen with lukewarm water. Cover with stiff paste made from approved *alkaline* stain remover. Or ask your druggist to recommend a biological washing powder that does *not* contain bleach. Keep poultice damp for two hours by covering with moistened cloth. Scrape off paste. Rinse well with clear water. While damp, brush in direction of pile with medium-soft nylon or bristle brush. Air-dry thoroughly away from direct heat.
Chewing gum	Cool gum with ice wrapped in plastic bag. When gum is cold, scrape off as much as possible. Then use white spirit or a chewing-gum remover approved by the National Institute of Rug Cleaners. Finish by making solution of crystallizing shampoo or baby shampoo. Add 1 teaspoon white vinegar per pint. If using baby shampoo, rinse

Stain	Remedy
	well with clear water. While damp, brush in direction of pile with medium-soft nylon or bristle brush. Air-dry thoroughly away from direct heat.
Coffee or tea	As quickly as possible, flush stain with plain soda water, blotting with white paper towel each time. Then make solution of baby shampoo. Add 1 teaspoon white vinegar per pint. Rinse well with clear water. While damp, brush in direction of pile with medium-soft nylon or bristle brush. Air-dry thoroughly away from direct heat.
Liquid shoe polish	Wipe gently with white spirit or similar solvent. Make solution of crystallizing shampoo or baby shampoo. Add 1 teaspoon white vinegar per pint. If using baby shampoo, rinse well with clear water. While damp, brush in direction of pile with medium-soft nylon or bristle brush. Air-dry thoroughly away from direct heat.
Solid shoe polish	Wipe gently with white spirit or similar solvent. Make solution of crystallizing shampoo or baby shampoo. Add 1 teaspoon white vinegar per pint. If using baby shampoo, rinse well with clear water. While damp, brush in direction of pile using medium-soft nylon or bristle brush. Air-dry thoroughly away from direct heat. If stain remains, repeat the process.

STORING RUGS

Oriental rugs (for that matter, all precious textiles) should be stored either flat or rolled. Folding woolen rugs for a week or two should do no harm but if they are left that way for long periods they will become badly creased. If any friction has taken place, the wool along the edges of the crease may be damaged. Very thick rugs, such as Persian Bijars, should never be folded because this tends to break their foundation threads.

Never, ever store a rug before you are sure it is free of moths. Choose a cool dry place. Lay the rug on its face and liberally dust the back with camphor powder. Then turn the rug face up and cover it with a large sheet of plain brown paper, or tissue paper if you prefer. (Do not use newspapers as the print could stain the rug.) Sprinkle the paper with more camphor powder. Next you need a round wooden pole or cardboard tube that is approxi-

A Seraband Mir Saruk rug. Saruks are often thick, and like Bijars, they should be stored flat to avoid damaging their foundation threads.

mately the same length as the width of the rug. The tube will prevent the rolled rug from being bent and straining its foundation threads. Making sure there are no creases, roll up both the rug and the paper around the tube. Try to make sure that the paper separates the camphor powder from the face of the rug. So that the pile doesn't get squashed, roll the rug quite loosely, *against* the pile. Then wrap the whole roll in a sheet of clean dry plastic, sprinkled with yet more camphor powder. Loosely tie up the bundle with string, leaving the ends open to allow air to circulate. Seal the ends against moths in the summer months but remember to open them again in the fall.

If you prefer to store your rugs flat, spread a large sheet of clean dry plastic and sprinkle it with camphor powder. Place the rug on top, face up, and cover it with a sheet of brown paper. Sprinkle the paper with more camphor powder and lay your second rug on top of this, continuing for as many rugs as you have to store. The bottom sheet of plastic must be large enough to fold over the entire stack. Fold the plastic quite loosely. Be sure to seal the seams with sticky tape to keep moths out during the summer and remember to undo them in the fall to let in the fresh air.

Using either of these methods, your rugs can be safely stored indefinitely. Just be sure that they are kept cool and completely dry and renew the camphor powder once a year when you check the rugs.

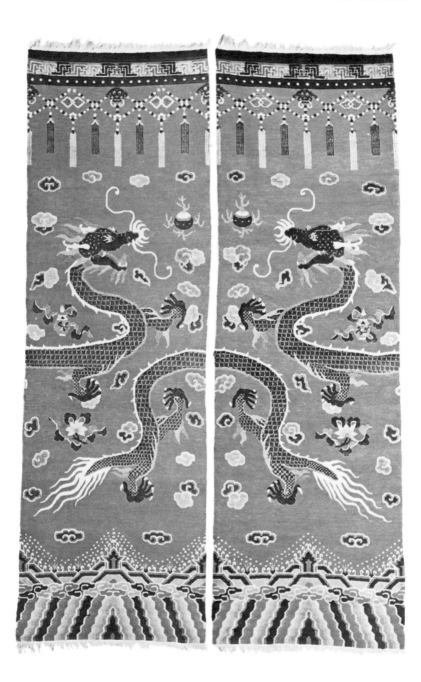

Chinese pillar rugs made to be folded around a pillar so that the two long sides come together and the dragon appears to encircle the pillar.

CHAPTER SEVEN

The Antique Tangle

Old is relative. To a geologist it may be two hundred million years, to a teen-ager it may be thirty years and to a biologist, old may be just three days.

In the world of oriental rugs "old" is also relative. To the seller, a rug is older; to the buyer, the same rug is not so old. This situation comes about for two reasons. Firstly, it is virtually impossible to pinpoint the exact year in which a rug was made; therefore, a range is more appropriate. Secondly, all other things being equal, *age means money*. Consequently, many descriptive terms have evolved over the years, especially on the retail level. Today in a *retail* store, a rug's age may be described along any of the lines of the following table:

Antique	50 years and older
Semi-antique	30 to 99 years old
Old	20 to 99 years old
Semi-old	10 to 50 years old
Used	1 to 10 years old
New	0 to 5 years old

The ranges are all slanted in favor of the rugs sounding as old as possible.

A general guide as to the reputability of a store is their use of the term "semi-antique"—reliable rug stores seldom describe any rug as semi-antique. Instead, they prefer to follow the descriptions commonly used in the *wholesale* rug trade:

Antique	100 years or more
Old	40 to 99 years
Semi-old	20 to 39 years
New	0 to 19 years

As you see, even for the trade, the ranges are approximate. Only the scientist in his laboratory can be more precise.

The description, "antique, over one hundred years old," is the only one that possesses some authenticity: one hundred years is the age that qualifies a rug for duty-free importation into the United States and many other countries. So a certificate from the store worded in this way is helpful (but not binding) if you are bringing the rug through customs duty-free.

One of the wholesale merchants I know has a favorite expression that he uses whenever he is asked the age of a rug. Smiling broadly, he says, "Old enough." I used to find this incredibly unhelpful in the days when I was trying to learn the rudimentary facts about rugs. Now, of course, I realize that he is right. If a rug is "old enough" to have acquired a lustrous patina and glowing mellowed colors (provided that the rug is in good condition), does it really matter what age it is? As long as you are not being asked to pay extra just because it is "antique," there is no serious disadvantage to a rug being eighty instead of one hundred years old. On the contrary, it will look much the same, wear a bit longer and should cost you less money. You won't be paying the premium that is part of the reason for the high prices asked for antiques.

So, in this valley of vagueness, how do we begin to determine the old from the new, the antique from the not-so-antique? Unlike furniture, where frequent changes of style are dictated by fashion, oriental rugs have altered very little over the centuries. The process of weaving by hand is basically the same now as it has always been; the designs are almost always traditional ones; and the sheep haven't changed much either. So what we need to do is hunt for clues if we want to know the approximate age of a rug.

Clue Number One: Color

The range of colors makes a good starting point. The range that can be made using pure vegetable dyes is comparatively limited.

Kashgai nomads weaving on a horizontal loom as their tribe has done for centuries.

You can easily become familiar both with these colors and with the effects of time on vegetable dyes just by looking at collections of antique rugs in museums. As I have explained in Chapter 3, reliable synthetic dyes were not available until the late 1920s. The aniline-dyed rugs have deteriorated to such an extent that there are very few of them left to confuse you. If in doubt, do the handkerchief test; aniline smells very nasty on the handkerchief. So, if the colors are obviously timeworn, vegetable ones, you have found your first clue.

Another way you can find out whether or not the colors in a rug are genuinely old is with the aid of a magnifying glass. The pile of old rugs in which time has softened the dyes has a smooth gradation of color from the base of the knot to the paler top of the tuft. If, when you break open the pile, the magnifying glass reveals a mid-tone band of color approximately halfway up the tufts, then you may be sure that the aging of the colors has

The mid-tone band of color halfway up the tuft is clearly delineated if the rug has been "enhanced."

been "enhanced" by the use of various kinds of bleach applied after the rug was removed from the loom, and that the rug is not genuinely old.

Clue Number Two: Type of Rug

The type of rug is also important in determining age. Many varieties of rugs have only come into existence in this century. If, for example, you know that a rug was made in Pakistan, it won't be an antique because Pakistan only started producing rugs after World War II. Similarly, all the thick, heavy types of Indian and Chinese rugs are modern. The Persian Qum rugs have all been made in the last sixty years or so, as have the Persian "white" Kashans. (These are actually ivory, robin's-egg blue or pale green, but the trade has labeled them all "white.") White Kashans were only made after 1920, in response to the Western markets' demands for pale rugs. The pastel-colored Taba-Tabriz rugs are another example of Persia's efforts to please the Western buyers who wanted, in addition to pastel colors, thicker rugs than Tabriz had been making. The "Persian design" Romanian rugs, which are made in the state-owned workshops, appeared on the scene less than thirty years ago. Antique Kashmir rugs are also unknown (the so-called antique Kashmirs were actually made in the Khorasan area of Persia).

Other examples are the Indian Agras. In spite of the fact that they share the famous name of those rugs made in and around Agra's jail (the prisoners with long sentences wove enormous rugs), the modern-day Agras are quite different. Just like that of the new Pakistani pieces, their wool is soft and is artificially given a shiny look. Modern Agras copy the Persian designs, in particular those of Kashan and Tabriz (Pakistan tends to concentrate on the Bokhara/elephant's-footprint designs of the Turkomans and the Turkish Ghiordes-style prayer rugs). Both the new Agras and the Pakistani rugs can be recognized by their floppiness and their distinctive sturdy white cotton fringes. As none of the above-mentioned rugs can yet be antique, you have now narrowed the field considerably.

Clue Number Three: Size of Rug

The size of a rug can give you a clue as to possible antiquity. For instance, if the rug you are looking at was made in or near the Persian town of Heriz, it's worth remembering that until about

A "white" Kashan rug, circa 1960.

1870 almost all Heriz rugs that were made were keleys (the long, narrow rugs mentioned in Chapter 2).

Old and antique Persian Khorasans are also usually keleys. (If they have a design in each corner rather like a long-necked bird's head, they probably are over one hundred years old.) Since the beginning of this century, far fewer keleys have been made in Persia. These sizes are now unpopular because they do not suit the layout of our Western homes.

Clue Number Four: Change of Style

Changes in the style of a particular type of rug can be helpful when you are trying to date it. For example, it is extremely rare for a late-eighteenth-century or early-nineteenth-century Isfahan to have been woven on a foundation of any material other than cotton and to have a knot count above 400 per square inch. On the other hand, the fine modern Isfahans (made in Isfahan, not Meshed—see Chapter 8) are almost always woven on a silk warp and weft and their average knot counts are considerably higher.

Rugs woven in the Hamadan region also show a change of style. In the old days, in the villages of this area, the Persian weavers frequently made rugs with camel-colored backgrounds. Modern-day Hamadans seem to use every color under the sun, except camel. The softly multicolored, glowing Mouteshan Kashan rugs are no longer made. These days, Kashans are made in the traditional style, including the white ones.

When a rug is made of silk, no matter from which country it originates, if it is antique the silk will be of a high quality. Slub silk was unknown until this century, as was art silk (mercerized cotton). Rugs woven from straightforward cotton always have a matted look if they are antique.

If the rug you are examining is an Anatolian (Turkish) one and you want to know whether it is antique, look at the weft threads. If these turn out to be red, that's an important clue: most of the antique Anatolians have red weft threads, and their weave tends to be rather coarse (less than 100 knots per square inch). Coarse knotting (even as low as 40 per square inch) is also typical of antique woolen Chinese pieces. In this case, the coarser the weave, the older the rug is a very general rule.

It is also worth keeping in mind that the phrase "antique style" does not mean that a rug is antique.

Clue Number Five: Woven Dates

Dates woven into a rug can give you a clue as to when it was made, so long as you understand them. Chronologically, the Moslem calendar begins with the year of Mohammed's flight from Mecca in A.D. 622 and is based on the lunar year. Our Gregorian calendar, named after Pope Gregory XIII (who in 1582 updated Julius Caesar's calendar), is based on the solar year. So we need to do a couple of easy calculations if we want to translate the Moslem dates on oriental rugs to our own system.

First, you *divide* the Moslem date by 33. Next, *subtract* the resulting number from the Moslem date. Then, *add* 622 (the year of Mohammed's flight). For example, if the Moslem date on a rug was 1190, the arithmetic would be as follows:

1190 ÷ 33 = 36 (rounded off to the nearest whole number)

1190 − 36 = 1154

1154 + 622 = 1776

A much more tricky problem is to read the Moslem date in the first place. The writing varies considerably. In the table below, I have illustrated the most prevalent versions in use today:

The date on a rug only tells us approximately how old it is. The weavers seldom receive a formal education and so most of them are unable to read or write. Therefore, they will often copy the designs of dates they see around them or dates that are woven into other rugs. Besides, even if a weaver is literate, we are still left with the question whether the chosen date reflects the year in which a rug was begun or the year in which it was finished. Nevertheless, there is a certain romance in knowing that you are walking on a rug made about the time when Napoleon was courting Josephine, 1796 (1211 = ١٢١١), Florence Nightingale was carrying her lamp, 1854 (1271 = ١٢٧١) or Custer was fighting his battle at the Little Big Horn, 1876 (1293 = ١٢٩٣).

Just to make sure that a date is the original one put there by the weaver, carefully examine the wool and the weaving around it. If a date has been falsified, it is usually the second numeral from the left that is altered, adding ninety-seven years to a rug's apparent age, encouraging you to believe that it is antique.

Antiques directly involve us with the past and reassure us about the future. Besides, in a practical way, we can reason that if a rug has lasted for more than a hundred years, it must be a good one.

HOW TO CHECK THE CONDITION
OF OLD RUGS

When you are considering buying an old or antique rug, it is very important to check its condition.

CRACKING: First of all, check to see if it is rotten, or "cracking," as the trade describes it. To do this, lay the rug on its face and look at the back to see if there are any light-colored patches. If there are, these could be the first signs of mildew, so you should pay special attention to them as you proceed with the test. Fold the rug across first in one direction and, after testing it, again in the other direction. Listen carefully as you twist the rug *gently* but firmly, gripping it in both hands. Stop the instant you hear any staccato splitting sounds. They are the foundation threads snapping as the rug breaks up. I have never knowingly sold a rug that was cracking, and I would strongly suggest that you never buy one. *Do* remember to ask the dealer's permission before you begin this test; if he won't let you do it, don't buy.

Rugs that should *not* be tested in this way are the thick, heavy, tightly woven pieces such as Persian Bijars. Their fine, fragile cotton weft threads could be seriously damaged by folding even if the rug is brand new. In these cases, you will either have to put your trust in the dealer (which, if you have chosen wisely, is an excellent solution) or select another type of rug.

After a rug has passed the "cracking test" (if it fails, forget it), the next step is to feel the material. Silk should not be brittle, no matter how old it is. It should always feel soft and smooth. Wool, on the other hand, will vary considerably with age. As wool grows older, its lanolin content becomes depleted, and although a woolen rug that has been polished by the tread of stockinged feet may *look* like silk, it will *feel* quite firm and sometimes even bristly. An old or antique rug will often seem rather gritty when you feel it between your fingers, particularly on the reverse side. (The *only* new rugs that have this type of gritty feeling are those from the Senneh area in Persia.)

KNOTS: Another clue is the appearance of the knots when seen from the back of the rug. Old knots will have been flattened out and slightly polished as the rug was being walked on. Breaking open the pile on the face of the rug can help you to know whether or not it is an old piece, for no matter how thoroughly the rug may have been cleaned, the cotton foundation threads will have become discolored, often a yellowish gray, if the rug is very old.

REPAIRS: A quick and easy way to spot repairs is to run your hand over both the front and the back of the rug. Mended areas feel rough and bumpy. If you then look very closely, you will see the extent of the work. Not all bumps are made by repairs. They could be due to a patch of uneven clipping of the pile. However, if the rug is an old one, nine times out of ten you will find that the bump is due to a mend. The technique of weaving is relatively simple and is, therefore, quite simple to repair. If the work has been done by a professional who takes pride in the job and who uses correctly dyed and appropriately weathered wools, then you should not allow small repairs to bother you. When the wools have *not* been weathered, the coloring of the repaired areas can change over the years so that they really do begin to show. If you have any doubts about the quality of the work, try to reach an agreement with the dealer that, if this should ever happen, the repair would be redone for you free of charge. Minor professionally done repairs, while they have little effect on either the value or the durability of rugs, do make a useful bargaining point, as I have indicated in Chapter 8.

To spot unrepaired holes or thin areas in an old rug, ask the dealer to hold it up so that a strong light (bright daylight is ideal) can shine directly through it. Don't be surprised or disappointed if you find one or two holes or weak places. Most old rugs have suffered from either moths or harsh treatment at one time or another in their lives. Providing the dealer agrees to have the holes properly mended and the weak patches strengthened, you needn't worry about them. Just be sure to check the rug over when the job is done. Reputable dealers examine all their old rugs before offering them for sale but it's possible to miss noticing a small hole in an intricate pattern, and the dealers should gladly pay the cost of repairing it.

When you are buying your rug through a broker from large wholesale warehouses, the situation is slightly different. The trade people work on small profit margins and they handle huge numbers of rugs. Often, the first chance they get to check a rug over is when you decide that you like it. If repairs are needed, they will naturally arrange for the work to be professionally done, but it's possible that you may be asked to pay the cost of the repair.

WEAR PATTERNS: Aside from actual holes or repairs, it is also important to notice the wear patterns on old rugs. They should be as even as possible so that the pile is approximately the same length over the whole face of the rug. As usual, there is an exception—those parts of the pattern where the wool has been eroded by acid in the dye. Black and dark brown are the two colors which you will frequently find eaten away like this, producing an embossed look. Sometimes this happens to rugs that are only twenty years old.

Because a rug *looks* old does not mean that it *is*. If it has been mistreated, any rug may be torn and tattered after only a decade or two. Whereas, if the rug has been well treated and especially if it has hung on a wall for years, an antique, hundred-year-old piece may appear to be almost new. A useful test is to pick one of the knots from the back with a pin (do remember to ask for the dealer's permission). Then, smooth out the knot and, as you release it, notice how fast it curls up again. The faster the curl, the older the rug. A similar test is to draw out a weft thread and soak this in a glass of water for a day or two. When you take it out of the water, if the weft is old it still won't be straight; if it's not so old, it will be.

PAINTED PIECES: It also helps to be aware that many old, worn rugs are painted to restore their colors and designs. This can be a good solution when the cost of repiling would be more than the rug is worth, but I would not advise you to buy an expensive antique that has been painted. In some cases, paint is used to create a whole new design, so that when you compare the design on the face of the rug with the one on the reverse side, you may discover that they don't match up. The handkerchief test can be most useful in detecting painted pieces.

REDUCED RUGS: When you are buying an old or antique rug, do check to see that it's all there. A lot of old pieces have been "reduced." This means that the fringes and borders are cut off when they become worn, a process which costs far less money and time than doing a reweave. If the rug is not expensive, reduction is not something to worry about. However, if you are paying a high price, then I feel that you should at least be getting the entire rug. Looking carefully at the overall design will soon show you if the pattern is lopsided or if the side borders fail to match up with the end ones. Telltale color at the base of the fringe, just where it meets the rug, is a sign that the ends of the rug have been reduced. When rugs are originally washed to clean them, small amounts of excess dye may have stained the warp threads beneath the pile as the dye was being flushed away. The line of color on the cotton fringe is a sign that the original fringe wore out and was replenished by fraying out part of the rug itself. If a false fringe has been added, look underneath it to make certain that the weft threads have been sewn in place and the rug is not quietly unraveling. If the candys (side cords) seem newer than the rest of the rug, they have probably been replaced. This doesn't matter at all if the reason they were renewed was because they were worn out. New candys can be a sign that part of a border has been reduced. Just studying the design for a while will tell you if the rug is all present and correct.

COUNTERFEIT ANTIQUES

The consistent demand for antique oriental rugs in the West and the fact that, as I mentioned, age means money, is why "counterfeit antiques" enjoy a flourishing market. The finest pieces have always been too expensive to tamper with but virtually every other type of rug has been threatened. To realize the high prices that the Western countries will pay for antiques, both in Turkey and in Persia, perfectly good new rugs are quite literally burned, buried and battered in order to "antique" them. A favorite method is to lay the rugs in the road and allow the traffic to damage them. The surface of the pile is grazed by the wheels of the trucks driving over the rugs; their foundation threads are nonked in the mine of pulling donkeys, camels and other animals; and children join in the destructive game by deliberately trampling and scuffing the rugs into the dirt with their feet.

A guide as to whether or not a rug has received this treatment is to scrutinize the back with a magnifying glass. As I have said, unless a rug has spent most of its life hung on a wall or draped over a chest, the back of a genuinely antique rug will be quite smooth and the knots will be flattened. The backs of rugs that have lain in the roadway for only a few weeks will still have little fibers of wool attached to them. Occasionally, these fibers are singed off, but then the rugs have a burnt smell which lingers for years.

Another antiquing technique is to make holes in the rugs by scraping them with a brick. When the holes are obvious enough, they are crudely mended. Coffee grounds are often rubbed into the pile to dull the bright colors. Alternatively, rugs may be buried in shallow holes in the ground; if the ground is damp and the rugs are left there long enough, mildew can set in and begin to rot the foundation threads.

In one town that I visited, I went exploring and found a group of men diligently "antiquing" in a sunny concrete yard. The center of the yard was occupied by a rectangular pool with sloping sides which were festooned with rugs. Before being laid out in the sun to dry, the rugs were soaked in the water of the pool to which a considerable quantity of lime was added. The effect of this lime-wash, coupled with the intensified sunlight reflected off the water, drastically bleached the colors of the rugs. When a rug was sufficiently faded, it would be held up while both the back and the front were scorched with a blowtorch. Wool is slow to burn, so instead of completely destroying the rug, the flame burned away only the top surface of the wool. This gave it a dry, withered appearance. Finally, the rug was spread on the ground and, using a big iron file, one of the men scraped away some of its pile. Handfuls of dirt were rubbed into the bald patches and the "antique" was then ready for sale.

This type of treatment is one of the reasons I have suggested that you check to see if the wear pattern is fairly uniform. If it is, the rug is likely to be more serviceable and you can be relatively sure that its pile was not deliberately removed. (Plain, unpatterned areas of rugs tend to be left undamaged, perhaps because the bald patches would look so ugly that, "antique" or not, nobody would want to buy them.)

The weavers who spend months and years creating these rugs are rarely involved in any "antiquing." When all is said and done, counterfeit rugs are still handmade oriental rugs; they have to be to survive this barbarous treatment.

AVAILABILITY OF ANTIQUE RUGS

Like a lot of other masterpieces, many of the best genuine antique rugs have now disappeared from the open market into museums and private collections around the world. Large numbers have been bought by the countries in which they were woven to preserve examples of their national heritage. For the same reason, many governments have introduced laws prohibiting antiquities from leaving the country. Even so, it is still possible to buy good antique rugs at prices that are not too astronomical. Among the best buys are:

- Baluchis (Persian)—nomadic, often prayer rugs
- Bokharas (Turkoman)—seminomadic
- Hamadans (Persian)—village
- Kelims (Afghanistan, Persian, Russian, Turkish)
- Mongolian rugs
- Tibetan rugs
- Various tent bags, saddlebags, camel and horse trappings, etc.

An example of a fine Tabriz rug, circa 1975.

Generally, these are all small sizes, which also helps to keep their prices reasonable.

Antique rugs can never become extinct, for one key reason. Year by year, antiques are "grown." The eighty- and ninety-year-old rugs of the 1970s become the antiques of the eighties and nineties. So why not *grow your own antiques,* have fun doing so and save money at the same time? Every now and then articles are written extolling antique rugs as being the only ones worth buying. I find it hard to understand such a narrow viewpoint and I suspect that it is due to two things: firstly, ignorance of the existence of the lovely *top-quality* new rugs which will certainly become the antiques of the future; and secondly, in the case of a few retail stores, price. The prices of the new rugs are relatively easy for the client to check up on in other stores.

Finally, it's worth remembering that oriental rugs are works of art. Posters are designed to have an instant appeal. Fine paintings, on the other hand, need time to be fully appreciated. In the same way, the longer you look at *good* rugs, the more you will see in them and the more beautiful and meaningful they will become for you. This is true whether the rug is one year or one hundred years old.

Arabesques on the dome of Masjid-i-Shah (the King's Mosque) in Isfahan, Persia.

CHAPTER EIGHT

Profit–Sharing

Acquiring a beautiful rug that you really want is an exciting and pleasurable experience. But getting that rug at a bargain price adds a dimension of triumph. The purpose of this chapter is to help you understand the bargaining process and to suggest ways in which you can develop your bargaining skills. If you successfully use the techniques that follow, you should be able to save 10, 20, 30 percent or more of the retail tag price of the rug. If you really dislike the whole idea of bargaining, your safest recourse is to buy through a broker, one you are sure you can trust. The broker will have used all the bargaining skills on your behalf so that the price is right before you begin choosing your rugs.

Assuming that you have accepted the challenge of buying a rug on your own, you should always be able to get *some* discount. It's only a matter of how much. We know that interior designers need only to show their calling cards to get 10 to 30 percent off the list price. Relatives of the dealer always seem to get a discount (the closer the relative, the higher the discount). You can always get something off (5 to 10 percent) for paying in cash instead of using a credit card. There are none of the fair-trading rules about oriental rugs that sellers of electrical appliances sometimes worry about. As with houses, used automobiles and antiques, the price of a rug is determined by what the market will bear. If it is a seller's market, discounts are smaller; if it is a buyer's market, discounts can be substantial.

If one thinks back to rug sales advertised in newspapers, figures of 33 to 50 percent off list price are not uncommon. Even at these discounted prices, sellers are not losing money—they're just making less. Unlike automobiles, appliances and other mass-produced items, handmade rugs do not lose their value with time. They appreciate, not depreciate. Therefore, rugs are never sold below cost (except in extremely rare circumstances such as bankruptcy or a private sale—but even these may not be wholly legitimate). Now, if a seller can make money after giving up to 50 percent off list price, you know that there is a large bargaining range available. Your task is to get as much of that range as you can.

There are three categories of rug buyers:

1. The buyer whose attitude is "money is no object." He or she may be exceedingly wealthy or caught in a situation where bargaining is out of the question (e.g., not wanting to give the impression of being a cheapskate in front of a close companion). If you are in this category, pay the price and skip the rest of this chapter.

2. The buyer who has no time to bargain or is too embarrassed to try. If you are in this category, my suggestion is to take a deep breath, offer 20 percent below list price and take 10. If the seller insists on the full price, offer cash for the 10 percent discount. If still no deal is made, you have a choice of either walking out (the seller may call you back and agree to your offer) or paying the full price.

3. The buyer who feels he or she would like to bargain or would like to learn how or would just like to save some money. If you are in this category, read on.

Most retail buying in the United States is conducted on a take-it-or-leave-it basis. Prices are marked, giving an apparent legitimacy to the numbers. We are taught to believe that the prices quoted are fair, reasonable and unalterable. But this is not true in most other parts of the world. I have bargained for shoes in Italy, a taxi ride in Turkey, a suit in England and a meal in Greece—things we would not dream of negotiating for in America. Rugs, however, are one of the few exceptions. Why? Perhaps it's because they originate in countries where bargaining is·a way of life. Rugs pass through the hands of exporters, importers and wholesalers who, more times than not, come from the same array of countries and are accustomed to bargaining when *they* are buying. Only when the rugs reach the retail stores in America do the prices become "fixed," and customers are expected to pay the listed price because that is the accepted way of doing things here.

Bargaining is a win/lose process. Every dollar you save is a dollar in your pocket. Conversely, every dollar the seller saves is a dollar out of your pocket. For example, if the tag price of a rug is $1,000 and you buy it for $750, you have saved $250 and the seller has lost $250. Bargaining is a competitive process based on power. You cannot persuade most sellers to lower their prices because they like you; you must maneuver them into it by using your power base. To this extent, bargaining is like a chess game involving a series of moves.

Research conducted in recent years on the bargaining process has come up with some interesting findings:

- Persons going into the bargaining process with high aspiration levels do significantly better than those who have more modest aspirations: "I'm going to go into that store and buy that rug for 40 percent off the tag price."
- Large initial demands (a very low offer) improve the probability of getting a significant discount: "The rug lists at $1,000. I'm willing to pay $800. I will first offer $600."
- Persons who yield in small amounts do better: "I offered $600, the seller countered with $900. I will now offer $650."
- Quick settlements result in extreme outcomes and usually favor skilled bargainers: You offer $600; the seller counters with $950. You get uncomfortable and want to get out of the bargaining situation, so you offer $900. The seller sees your impatience and sticks to $950, to which you agree. In less than a minute, the bargaining is over. You leave feeling you gained $50 when, in fact, you probably lost $100.

There are three primary factors in successful negotiating that I call the AIM of bargaining:

A—Attitude (the secret of bargaining)
I—Information (the foundation of bargaining)
M—Methods (the skill of bargaining)

ATTITUDE

Having the right attitude is the secret of successful bargaining. If you are a person who will do almost anything to avoid failure, you will probably pay the quoted price for a rug or walk out of the store. If, however, you are willing to take a risk (and possibly lose), you have the right attitude to be a successful bargainer.

Attitude is a state of mind. If you ask five-year-old children if they can paint, all of them will say yes. If you ask adults the same question, most of them will say they don't have the talent. To be a successful bargainer, you must believe that bargaining is not only possible, but that it is the only way to arrive at a fair price. You cannot make assumptions that undermine this attitude (for example: "He'll never sell us that rug for $700"). Here are three rules which will help fortify your attitude towards bargaining:

1. The quoted price is assumed to be the legitimate price and we tend not to question it. But the quoted price is, in reality, the seller's *maximum* price. If the rug is on sale, that *new price* becomes the seller's maximum price.
2. Don't be influenced by sales tactics such as
   price lists showing seller's costs
   price tags that are marked down
   a quick 5 percent off if you buy right now
   prices are going up next week
   another customer wants to buy it tomorrow
   it's the last one of its kind—there are no more.
3. Think of bargaining as a game—a game in which you can save your hard-earned money and at the same time learn a valuable skill.

Once you have established a positive attitude towards bargaining, an attitude that says "it is proper to bargain" and "I can and will bargain," it is time to examine two fundamental components of that attitude: *aspirations* and *power*.

As I mentioned before, there is ample research to show a direct relationship between how well people do in a bargaining situation and their aspiration level: people who expect more, get more. This is true in most aspects of our lives, but it works exceedingly well in bargaining for rugs. Aim higher and your outcome will be better, providing: you accept the risks; you do your homework; you are patient. This does not mean that you will finally settle on your "aspiration price." It means that your outcome will be better if you begin with high aspirations. "Reach for the sun and you will get the moon" is a good maxim when bargaining. There is a limit, of course, and the rule of thumb I use is "Ask for more (a lower price) than you're likely to get, but stay credible."

The second component of the attitude factor is power, *your* power. The seller's concept of your power is not how much you actually have, but how much he or she *thinks* you have. Your attitude will have a great bearing on this. Actual or perceived power will significantly improve your bargaining success. On the other hand, if you feel that the seller has all the power, you are in a poor bargaining position and will not do as well. So, to a large extent, bargaining is based on power—your power, as the seller sees it; and the seller's power, as you see it. You both have some, and I shall attempt to show you that you have more than you think you do.

We have a tendency to focus on the seller's power, ignoring our own. Here is a checklist of power sources I use to maintain my positive attitude and psychological power base. I'm sure you can add to it.

The seller's competition—
be aware of rugs, prices, credit, discounts, etc., in other stores.

Legitimacy—
believe in the concept that it is right, fair and reasonable to expect "something off" the initial price quoted.

Commitment to your goal—
do not just hope or wish, but be committed to obtaining a proper discount.

Knowledge
do your homework, plan, learn about rug values, the store, other customers' experiences, the authority of the salesperson, etc.

Risk-taking—
realize that there is power in knowing you can walk out and leave the deal "on the table." If the seller doesn't call you back, you can always come back another time or buy somewhere else.

Time—
accumulate power through the time the seller "invests" in you—showing you rugs and explaining things; know the time when the seller needs to sell, such as the end of the month or year if the seller needs to turn over his stock to pay creditors, landlord, staff or wholesalers.

Money—
know that the seller wants enough of your money to make a profit—that's his business. (How *much* profit he makes is your business.)

Be friendly—
use the power in your smile, your nice comments, your pleasant approach. It is difficult for the seller to get upset with you when you're friendly, even though you are bargaining hard.

Displaced power—
say "I understand your position, but my husband/wife holds the checkbook and he/she just won't go that high."

Ignorance—
say "I know you've tried to explain why this rug is so valuable but I just don't understand. I'm willing to pay $750 for it because I like it."

Bargaining skill—
capitalize on the fact that the seller usually encounters customers with little or no bargaining skill. By the time you finish this chapter and practice a bit, you will be able to surprise him.

INFORMATION

Having the necessary information is the foundation of successful bargaining. Information can be divided into information you give and information you get. Perhaps the most important rule to remember concerning giving information is: Don't. *Don't volunteer information.* Knowing your motives, your time pressures, how much money you have available, etc., all adds to the seller's power base. How can you bargain if you've told the seller that you just love that rug, the color and size are perfect, you need it tomorrow for your wife's birthday and have saved $1,000 for her present?

Whether you are buying a brass object in the bazaar in Morocco or buying a used automobile at your local car dealer's, the key question the seller will ask is "How much are you willing to pay?" or "How much would you like to spend?" He is fishing for information and it is prudent not to tell him. (Can you imagine getting a straightforward, honest answer from the seller if you asked him, "How much did this cost you?" Most sellers will not tell you, and if they do you still can't be sure it's the truth.) Once you have told him your maximum figure, you have lost most of your bargaining power.

Here is a typical example I have witnessed countless times in bazaars around the world. An American couple on a tour is visiting a local bazaar. They have been told by all their friends that they should bargain for whatever they want, not pay the full price. After looking for a while, they finally see a brass box they like (the merchant also sees they like this particular box). One of the couple asks the merchant, "How much is this box?" The merchant replies, "Only $10 for this beautiful handmade box of solid brass." (He has paid about $1.75 and local buyers pay $3 or less.) The couple remember their friends' advice and reply, "$10 is too much!" The merchant counters with "How much will you give me?" The couple look at each other and one replies, "No more than $7." The merchant winces and says that $7 is impossible but, because he likes them, he'll take $8. The couple pay the $8 and leave triumphantly, having "bargained" and saved $2!

This episode is typical in bargaining when an unskilled bargainer gives away important information. In this simple illustration the statement "No more than $7" tells the merchant that his bottom selling price is $7 and his top selling price is still $10. At $7 he has already made $5.25 and his only decision is how much of the remaining $3 he should try for. So always remember, never give the seller any more information than is absolutely necessary.

We are now ready to explore the all-important area of gathering information. To decide what information is critical for you, it is worthwhile to review the bargaining process: Bargaining is negotiating in the area between the highest figure you are willing to pay and the lowest figure the seller is willing to accept.

Let's say that a rug is initially quoted at $1,000. You estimate that the lowest figure the seller would accept is $800. On the other hand, you would like to buy the rug for $750, but would be willing to go as high as $900, if *absolutely necessary*. Diagramming the situation would look like this:

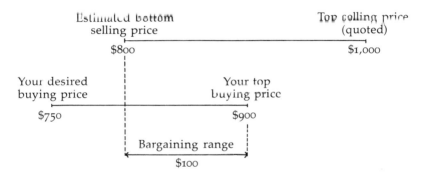

The bargaining range is between $800 and $900. Now, you're not negotiating on $1,000; you are bargaining on how much of the $100 you will get and how much the seller will get. Of course, this does not stop you from starting your bargaining at $600 and gradually moving up into your $750 to $900 range as the seller moves down from the $1,000 figure. The lower you start (providing the amount is credible) and the slower you move (small increments), the better chance you have of capturing the lion's share of the $100 in question. If you start high, say $800, chances are that you'll end up paying around $900 and losing most or all of the discretionary $100.

If the highest price you are willing to pay is lower than the lowest price the seller is willing to accept, then of course there is no bargaining range to work with and no deal is possible. Your choices then are: try again to get the seller down to your highest buying figure; raise your upper limit a little if the seller will come down a little; leave it for a while, try again in a few days; go somewhere else.

At this point there are three practical questions that need answering:

1. How do I determine my highest buying price?
2. How do I determine my lowest realistic price?
3. How do I determine my beginning bargaining offer?

If the seller is willing to move off the tag price at all (after some gentle nudging), you should have no problem getting at least a 10 percent discount. *Your highest buying price should be no more than 90 percent of the initially quoted or tag price of a rug.* In response to the statement "I sincerely want to buy the rug, but you've got to improve on the price," there is an excellent chance that the seller's first offer will be 10 percent off the tag price.

Assuming that the profit margin available to rug merchants at the retail level ranges from 50 percent to 100 percent, *your lowest realistic price should be about 75 percent of the quoted or tag price of a rug.* This 25 percent discount still allows the seller a healthy profit. For example, if a seller has bought a rug at $500 and prices it at $1,000 (a 100 percent profit margin) and you buy it at $750, the seller is making $250, or a 50 percent profit. If the merchant buys a rug at $667 and price tags it at $1,000 (a 50 percent profit margin) and you buy it at $750, the merchant is still making $83, or 12½ percent profit. Of course, many merchants use a profit margin higher than 100 percent and very few have profit margins as low as 50 percent, even during seasonal sales.

Your *beginning bargaining offer* should be lower than your lowest realistic price. It is your first thrust in the bargaining duel (the seller's first thrust is the tag price). If you have no other clues to go on, a good rule of thumb is to start at 60 percent of the initial asking price. This may upset the seller, but it is communicating two important points: (1) You are seriously interested in buying the rug; (2) you are not going to pay the full price. Because most customers do not bargain in America, the seller may react in one or more of the following ways:

- Argue that you have no idea of the value of the rug (this is irrelevant, but it shows the merchant still wants to sell the rug).
- Complain that the figure is below the seller's cost and you are being unrealistic.

- Try to sell you a cheaper rug in your "price range."
- Drop you as a potential customer.

Your response to any of these should be: "I sincerely want to buy the rug, but you've got to improve on the price."

We are now in a position to estimate three of the five figures involved in the bargaining situation—your highest buying price, your lowest realistic buying price, and your starting bargaining price. The other two figures are the seller's *highest selling price* and the seller's *lowest selling price*. The first of these two is easy to determine—it's the tag price or the first price quoted by the merchant. When you walk into a store and ask a salesperson the price of a rug, the answer is always the seller's highest selling price. This holds true even if the price is a sale price. For instance, a store may be advertising a 25 percent–off sale on all oriental carpets and a rug may have a tag price of $1,000 crossed out and $750 written in. The $750 is now the seller's maximum selling price.

The last of the two figures—the seller's lowest selling price—is the most difficult to determine and the most important. In fact, if you knew the seller's lowest selling price, there would be no need to bargain. All you would have to do is offer that figure and stick to it. But this is the one figure that you have the least information about. Some of the variables that the merchant uses in determining this figure are: the cost to the merchant of the rug; the rent of the store and other overhead expenses; the salaries of the staff; how badly the merchant needs cash; how long the rug has been in the shop; the merchant's judgment of the rug's value; the merchant's judgment of what you will pay; your potential as a future customer and so on.

Since the seller will never voluntarily disclose this figure to you at first meeting (just as you will not disclose your top buying figure at the beginning), you must make an intelligent guess. The more accurately you estimate this figure, the better your chance of bargaining successfully. During the bargaining process, you may revise your estimate upward or downward as you gather new information. For example, you see a rug in the window of a store with a sign saying "Special Price—$980." You've been looking for a rug of this size, design and color for some time and believe this could be just what you want. You are sure some discount is possible and you calculate the following:

Your highest buying price	$900 (this should be a firm figure)
Your lowest realistic price	$750 (this would be ideal)

Your first offer price $600 (this is an opening gambit)

The seller's highest price $980 (this is a given fact)

The seller's lowest price $800 (this is a first guess)

Diagramming these figures would look like this:

```
                            Seller's              Seller's
                          lowest price          highest price
                          ┝━━━━━━━━━━━━━━━━━━━━━━━┥
                            $800                    $980
                       (least known figure)

              Your lowest              Your highest
Your first offer  realistic price        buying price
┝━━━━━━━━━━━━━━━━━━┿━━━━━━━━━          ━━━━━━━┥
  $600             $750                        $900

                        ┆Bargaining range┆
                        ┝━━━━━━━━━━━━━━━━━┥
                              $100
```

At this point, the question is: "Who gets most of the $100 discretionary money—you or the merchant?"

You offer $600 cash for the rug in the window and the merchant becomes visibly upset. He explains that this is a $1,200 rug and that each week he puts a different piece in the window to bring in customers and a $600 figure is out of the question. He shows you the original price tag of $1,200 and explains that he paid much more than $600 a year ago for the rug and its value has gone up in twelve months. You feel a bit embarrassed and believe part if not all of his story. At this point you re-evaluate the seller's *lowest selling price* from your original guess of $800 to $850 and say, "I appreciate your situation, but to me it's not realistically worth more than $650." The situation can now be diagrammed as follows:

```
                            Seller's              Seller's
                          lowest price          highest price
                          ┝━━━━━━━━━━━━━━━━━━━━━━━┥
                            $850                    $980
                        (first estimate)

Your second     Your lowest                  Your highest
   offer       realistic price                buying price
┝━━━━━━━━━━━━━━━┿━━━━━━━━━           ━━━━━━━━━━┥
  $650          $750                            $900

                              Bargaining
                                range
                          ┝━━━━━━━━━━━━━━━━━┥
                                $50
```

Now the question is: "Who gets most or all of the $50 bargaining range—you or the merchant?"

In the illustration above, you revised upward your estimate of the merchant's lowest selling price based on new information you received *and* believed (from $800 to $850). On the other hand, different information may have caused you to re-evaluate downward from $800 to $750. For example, if when you offered $600 cash, the salesman left to talk with the manager and they both came back to talk to you, they would be indicating a very serious intention to sell the rug. This situation would be diagrammed like this:

	Seller's lowest price		Seller's highest price
	$750 *(second estimate)*		$980
Your first offer	Your lowest realistic price		Your highest buying price
$600	$750		$900
		Bargaining range	
		$150	

So, the one figure that you are more apt to change during the bargaining process is the seller's lowest price. Your revision will be based on the new information you have gathered through listening, observing, analyzing, probing and, above all, being patient.

Before leaving the subject of giving and getting information, it is worthwhile to list three important rules:

1. Ask probing questions that require more than just a yes or no answer:
   - If I want to sell the rug back to you in a year or so, would you buy it back, and if so, for how much?
   - Suppose the colors run when I clean it? What will you do for me?
   - What happens if it wears out in a year?
   - Why isn't my offer a fair and reasonable one?
   - Why is your price so high?
   - Do you have a similar rug a little smaller?
2. Don't interrupt when the seller is talking—listen, listen, listen:
   - You learn something.
   - The seller learns nothing.
   - You show interest, commitment.
   - The seller gets involved.
   - The seller feels he is getting your approval.
3. Once you set your highest buying price (and it is a *serious* error not

to), it must be firm—and never disclosed. Your highest buying price should be so definite that you would walk away before going above it. This will increase your power while bargaining. Disclosing your highest buying price (e.g., "I want to pay $750, but I can't go any higher than $900") gives away all your power. This seems quite obvious, but I've seen it happen over and over again.

METHODS

The various methods that can be used in the bargaining process require understanding and practice of the skill of bargaining. Some of the methods may be natural to you and require little practice but others may need some work. You can practice your bargaining methods in two ways: with people you know or with strangers.

First, role-play with your spouse or a friend. Pretend the other person is the merchant and "bargain" over a rug you already have in your home. Practice saying "The price is too high" and "I like the rug but you've got to do better on the price." Then try reversing the roles so that you put yourself in the salesperson's frame of reference. Role-playing may sound too simple to be worthwhile but I assure you that it will pay dividends: just saying the uncomfortable phrases out loud will help you when you have to say them again when they really count.

Second, practice with strangers. If it's against your nature to confront a salesperson with "The price is too high," you can practice this with a local butcher (not the one you rely on!) or in a clothing store. Gather up your courage, walk into the meat store and ask the price of a prime rib roast. Whatever price is quoted, say it's too high, smile and walk out. When you can do this without embarrassment, try it in a clothing store. The ultimate test is in a restaurant—after you have been seated and given the menu. When you can say, quite naturally, "The price is too high" and breeze out of a store or restaurant, it is time to try your hand at bargaining for an oriental rug. Here are some specific techniques you can use:

Getting the Merchant "On the Hook"

By definition, sellers want to sell, but it helps to get the merchant really interested in spending time selling to you. Remarking that

"We are going to furnish our new home with orientals instead of wall-to-wall carpeting; our first rug should be a good one" would excite any rug merchant.

Later in the negotiations statements such as "Yes, that's the rug I want—let's talk price" or "You've got a deal. I'll buy the rug—all we have to do is settle on a fair price" will convince the merchant that 95 percent of the sale has been made.

Showing your commitment to a specific rug will also raise the merchant's hopes of making a deal. You can do this by your actions: feel the rug, kneel on it, make the merchant lay it out in good light, turn it over, look for holes, repairs.

Using Two People

Having a second person with you can be helpful during the bargaining process providing some ground rules have been established between you. The first and most obvious rule is to settle on the rug you want before beginning price discussion. It will be difficult for you and the merchant to bargain on rug A if you and your spouse are arguing over whether you should buy rug A, rug B or rug C.

Once a specific rug has been decided on, I recommend that you agree that one person should be the buyer. This allows the other person to look and listen for cues, to observe the technique and attitude of the merchant and to concentrate on estimating the minimum price the merchant is willing to settle for. In other words, while the buyer is discussing *content* issues such as design, color, size, material, value, and price, the second person is watching the *process* issues: the merchant's interest, cooperativeness, firmness of voice and eye contact when mentioning price, eagerness to sell and so on.

I'm always amazed how a second person playing this role can pick up verbal cues not recognized by the person engaged in the main discussion. Here are actual examples of verbal cues that were ignored by buyers (and possible responses):

"The only person who could authorize a lower price is the manager."
(So let's talk to the manager.)
"I can't let this rug go much below this price." (So, how much is much?)
"I'm sure we can work this out." (So let's start—give me a fair price.)
"The boss would be very angry if I gave you a discount." (So, let him be angry—or let me talk directly to the boss.)
"It's our policy not to reduce prices except during advertised sales." (So make an exception.)

The Nice Guy/Tough Guy Technique

This technique seems so simple that it shouldn't work; but it does. A typical example would be a husband-and-wife combination where one plays the tough role and can bargain hard, be stubborn, growl a bit and generally appear uncooperative; the other person is the peacemaker, the compromiser, the cooperative and pleasant person the merchant likes to deal with. Whether the person playing the tough role walks out or just shuts up and sulks, the other person has the job of convincing the salesperson that some compromise must be arrived at to keep peace in the family and avoid outright divorce. The merchant thus ends up bargaining with someone he likes and sympathizes with and is consequently more vulnerable as the nice person attempts to arrive at a compromise solution.

Breaking the Impasse

Occasionally you and the merchant may find yourselves deadlocked during the bargaining process. Instead of the situation being allowed to polarize so that no further progress is possible, the impasse should be seen as a temporary slow-down and an attempt should be made to break through as soon as possible. When an impasse occurs, the first method I would recommend is to change the subject, preferably by asking a question. Here are some examples:

- What about underpadding for this rug? Do I need it?
- Do you know a good book on rugs that I can read?
- What about that rug on the wall? What kind is it?
- What if I buy two rugs instead of one—will I get a discount?
- If I pay cash, will I get a discount?
- What if I wait until after the holidays—can we make a deal then?
- What if I pick it up myself instead of having it delivered—how much will I save?
- What if I bring in some neighbors or relatives as customers? Will this help?

After a few minutes on the diversion issue try going back to the main subject. The change of pace may have helped to break the deadlock.

Another technique that may break the impasse is to change the buyer (if there are two of you) or change the seller (if there is more than one available). Different people have different personalities and the chemistry of the relationship will change when one of the individuals is replaced.

The third method is the most drastic but may be necessary when other techniques fail. This is to walk out, indicating, as you do so, that you really would like to buy the rug but the price is just a bit too high. Leaving your name and telephone number sometimes helps; it allows the seller to keep you as a potential customer and gives him time to think through the consequences of losing the sale. In effect, the slip of paper with your name on it continues to bargain for you after you have gone. You can always return at another time.

Getting the Extras

Although your primary goal is to obtain the rug you want at a good price, there are many little "extras" floating about that you may be able to get at no cost. The key is to know what they are and when to maneuver for them. Negotiating for the extras should usually begin *after* you have reached the rock-bottom price the seller will agree to and *before* you pay for the rug; otherwise the merchant has no incentive to give anything away (Of course, if the seller has already given you one or two extras during the bargaining process, so much the better.) This is also the time when the merchant has the strongest desire to close. He has made a deal and is anxious to collect. It is the optimal time to cash in on one or more extras.

Here are some extras to consider (I'm sure you will think of others as the situation develops):

- Free delivery (or credit if you pick up the rug)
- Free underpadding
- Free minor repairs to rug or fringes
- Free book on rugs (if being sold by merchant)
- Free cleaning (entire rug or spot)
- Written guarantee of what rug is (age, source, dyes, etc.)
- Written guarantee to buy back at same price
- No local tax (assume it was in negotiated price)
- Five percent off for check instead of credit card
- Ten percent off for cash (for a number of obvious reasons)
- Rounding off of the final figure ($1,215 rounded off to $1,200)

An extreme example I heard of—but one which I am in no way recommending—was an individual who bought a rug and agreed to pay on delivery. When the driver delivered the rug to the house, the individual gave him a check for 10 percent less than the agreed price. The driver telephoned the merchant and, after a good deal of discussion between the seller and the buyer, the rug was left at the discounted price.

Using Surprise Information

Occasionally, you may have a piece of information that would put the seller at a disadvantage. The trick is to use this information at the proper time. So, before you begin bargaining, review your special information and plan your strategy as to what would be the optimal time to surprise the seller. Here are some examples:

"The large department store downtown is having a one-third-off sale this week on all rugs—how much are you giving?"

"A neighbor of mine, Miss Jones, bought a rug from you last year and recently had it evaluated. They said it was worth less than she paid for it. That won't happen to me, will it?"

"I like the rug; I want to buy it—but I have only X amount of money in the bank. Is there anything we can do?"

"Three months ago this rug was in your window at $200 less than what you're asking now. Have you raised the prices of all your rugs?"

"You usually have a sale twice a year. When will your next one be? How much will this rug be when it is on sale?"

Using Deadlines

There are two kinds of deadlines—yours and the seller's. We tend to think about our own and sometimes we even impose deadlines upon ourselves (e.g., "I promised to buy the new rug for the holidays"). A good rule of thumb is to be prepared *not to buy* on the first visit. Also be aware of the seller's possible deadlines that I've given earlier in this chapter, such as salaries, rent, etc.

Trying for Closure

In any bargaining process there comes a time to try for closure. You and the seller may not have come to agreement but you're not too far apart and it may be worthwhile attempting to wrap it up. My suggestion is to say, "This is as high as I can go," and follow it with a statement such as:

"I'll write you a check right now."
"I have the cash with me."
"If you agree on this rug, let's look for a second one."

If this approach doesn't work and you feel continued discussion would prove fruitless at this time, I suggest you leave the shop, saying politely, "I've gone as far as I can go," and follow it with a statement like:

"I'll try the wholesale district in New York City."
"I'm going to look in other stores."
"We'll have to settle on a piece of furniture instead."

It wouldn't surprise me if the seller called you back and began negotiating again. If not, you can always come back another day.

The Take-It-or-Leave-It Response

What do you do when the salesperson won't budge off the listed price and, in effect, says "take it or leave it"? This takes some on-the-spot analysis of the motivation of the salesperson. There are at least three possible reasons for this response:

1. The person is only a sales clerk doing what he or she has been told to do, without any authority to alter prices.
   Solution: Ask to see the manager, and start again.
2. The salesperson is using this method as a tactic and believes you will eventually give in and pay the full price.
   Solution: Test it—say that it's too high and start to walk off. If you get no response, leave. You can always go back later.
3. The seller believes he can get top price from someone else in the near future; i.e., it's a seller's market.
   Solutions:
   • Try offering "cash on the table" less 10 percent, explaining that it is all you have to spend.
   • Ask about a discount if you buy two rugs. If the merchant is willing to drop the price for two, you know he can go down on one.
   • Look for defects or mistakes (coloring, repairs, size distortion, wrinkles). These could give the seller a face-saving way of reducing the price.
   • Go somewhere else.
   • If this is the only rug in the world you want, pay the full price.

In summary, if the salesperson won't budge after a number of attempts, you must analyze why and react accordingly.

A REVIEW LIST OF DOS AND DON'TS

Here is a list of items that are worth reviewing each time you enter into a bargaining situation. It will refresh your memory and help you focus on the areas where you feel least competent.

Don't be too anxious.
Don't talk too much.
Don't ask questions that will antagonize.
Don't be afraid to say "The price just isn't right."
Don't make the first concession.
Don't make consecutive concessions.
Don't yield in large amounts under pressure of a deadline.
Don't split the difference (if he gives $100, you give $50).
Don't interrupt an offer or the beginnings of an offer.
Don't let the seller interrogate you.
Don't interrogate the seller.
Don't get upset or angry.
Don't bargain in front of other customers.
Don't imply that the merchant is dishonest.
Don't argue with your spouse during negotiations (unless you are playing nice guy/tough guy).
Don't give up or take no for an answer easily.
Don't put down a deposit unless the receipt is marked "refundable."
Don't let the style of the store overwhelm you.

Do role-play; practice being tough, being the seller, walking out.
Do practice saying "That's too much" and "You've got to do better than that."
Do be pleasant and courteous.
Do settle on easy things first: "Do you take checks? Do you deliver? Will you store the rug for a few weeks?"
Do ask direct questions: e.g., "How long have you had this rug?"
Do listen; you can't learn anything while you're talking.
Do be patient; take your time.
Do take notes; it documents the process and slows you down.
Do stay with a theme: e.g., "I like the rug but the price is too high. Isn't there some way we can get together?"
Do leave yourself room to negotiate.

Do yield in small amounts; be stingy.

Do make it easy for the merchant to reduce the price: e.g., "The price is too high," *not* "Is that your final price?"

Do look for objections in the rug. List them (size, color, pattern, mistakes). The seller will give you reasons why the full price is justified; you should have reasons why it is not.

Do check your courage. If you're not sure, take no money, checks, credit cards with you on your first visit.

Do use "You've got to do better than that."

Do use one-upmanship: "Your competition is very busy" or "I read an article saying there soon will be a glut of rugs on the market."

Do final bargaining on off-peak hours, rainy or snowy days.

Do start with one rug even if you want two.

Do talk about two or three rugs even if you only want one.

A WORD OF CAUTION

In this chapter I have been discussing rug bargaining in legitimate shops and department stores, not in tourist traps. In many large cities there are stores that cater to out-of-towners, to the uninformed, to the gullible. They sell a variety of electronic items, watches, cameras and, often, rugs—both the handmade and the machine-made "oriental design" varieties. They start with high tag prices and volunteer large discounts; in effect, they do the bargaining for you. In ten minutes you will have reduced the price by as much as 50 percent and, if you buy, you will have a rug of questionable value. You will certainly have overpaid.

Only recently an individual told me how he "saved" 40 percent on a $1,200 rug in such a store in midtown New York City and they "threw in a camera and a digital watch as well." Another store nearby has a sign (apparently required by law) that reads: "Prices marked on all merchandise are above list." However, the sign is small, far above eye level on the wall. Discounts are easy to obtain here and, depending on how gullible the customer is, it should be possible to "bargain" the price down to the normal list price found in regular stores. Of course, rugs do not have list prices, but if this technique is being practiced on manufactured articles in the store, you can be sure that their rugs are being handled in the same way. The risks of buying rugs from such stores are high. I would strongly recommend that you go instead to responsible specialist oriental-rug stores or brokers who will always be there if you need them.

SUMMARY

Unlike most items we purchase, every oriental rug is bargainable. Your attitude towards what is a reasonable and fair price is a key ingredient in determining whether you will be an effective bargainer. High aspirations plus your power as seen by the seller lead to bargaining success.

Do your homework. Learn about rugs. Survey many stores. Determine your bargaining range. Don't give away key information. Do ask questions and then listen, listen, listen. Without a good information base you will be at a distinct disadvantage when bargaining with a skilled salesperson.

An effective bargainer uses many tactics during negotiations. The more skill you have in the various methods, along with your knowledge of when to use them, the more successful you will be as a bargainer.

As I mentioned at the beginning of this chapter, if you dislike the idea of bargaining, buy through a broker who will bargain for you. However, bargaining can be fun and the more you do it the easier it gets. It can also save you money—lots of it.

An Isfahan prayer rug woven from lamb's wool on a silk foundation. These rugs are becoming increasingly rare.

From Rugs to Riches

When I first entered the oriental-rug business, I was amazed at how the senior experts in the warehouses could accurately analyze and evaluate a rug in seconds. I knew it must have taken many years to develop this skill, beginning as a child learning from watching father or uncle working in the trade. Since people aren't born with this skill, I was determined to learn it. By asking questions, making mistakes, listening carefully, reading and asking more questions, I began to understand.

In this chapter I shall attempt to explain what I have learned about analyzing and evaluating oriental rugs. It is a complex subject involving thousands of different kinds of rugs with virtually infinite variations. In addition, prices keep changing because of political, economic and social forces throughout the world. By necessity, therefore, my explanation will be oversimplified. Nevertheless, it will be thorough enough to allow you to analyze the quality of almost all the rugs you are likely to encounter and to estimate their retail value.

ANALYZING A RUG

There is no precise formula for analyzing the "quality" of a rug. However, there are a number of criteria that can be examined which will give you definite indications as to whether a rug is of high quality, poor quality, or somewhere in between. These factors are: knots per square inch, material used, design, colors, age and condition.

The following tables will give you a method of analyzing a rug in terms of "value points" so that you can compare two completely different rugs using common factors. Later in this chapter we will convert these value points to money values by adding the key factor of country of origin.

As you go through the six tables determining value points on a specific rug, the tables for design, colors and condition may require you to *interpolate* the proper point number between two descriptions. For example, in the color table you may find the rug is better than the "2" description but not good enough to fit the "4" description. It would then receive a "3" rating.

You may find it difficult to use these tables if you are only familiar with one or two rugs (how can you compare designs or colors if you've only seen one rug?). I would recommend a visit to a good rug store or the rug department in a large store and spend some time examining a variety of rugs from inexpensive to very expensive. By looking at a dozen or so pieces across a wide range of quality, you will easily get an overall feel for color, design and material. This will make the descriptions in the tables more meaningful.

Factor 1: Knots

To measure this factor, turn over a portion of the rug and count the number of knots in a horizontal running inch (3 cm.). Do the same for a vertical running inch and multiply one number by the other. The resulting figure is the knots per square inch. You may wish to make your count in two or three places to obtain a good average, as the weave may vary from section to section. Remember that some rugs may have more than one row of knots squeezed in between the weft threads.

To determine the value points in the knots factor, use the following table:

TABLE 1

Knots per Square Inch	Value Points
729 and above	10
600–728	9
484–599	8
380–483	7
289–379	6
210–288	5
144–209	4

T A B L E 1—*Continued*

Knots per Square Inch	Value Points
91–143	3
49–90	2
21–48	1
20 and below	0

Factor 2: Materials

To measure this factor, determine the material used in the rug. Locate the description on the table below and record the value points. (Any wool that has undergone a strong chemical bleach should be classed, for the purposes of this table, as "poor wool.")

T A B L E 2

Material	Value Points
Silk pile on a silk warp	10
Fine kurk wool (lamb's wool) on a silk warp or a fine cotton warp	9
Fine wool with or without silk inlay on a fine cotton or silk warp; also silk on a cotton warp	8
Silk and good wool on a cotton warp	7
Good wool on a cotton warp	6
Regular wool on a cotton warp	5
Regular wool on a wool warp; regular cotton on a cotton warp	4
Cotton (art silk) on a cotton warp	3
Poor wool on a cotton warp	2
Poor wool on a jute warp	1
Cotton on a jute warp	0

Factor 3: Design

When you are allocating these value points, do remember that oriental rugs are handmade and therefore their designs are often legitimately less uniform than those of the machine-made rugs. For example, a row of matching flowers need not be identical. The following table is based on two key elements: one is the amount of background field that has been left undecorated (the less decoration, the lower the rating); the second is the intricacy and precision with which the design has been drawn. If a whole design is drawn so that it is seriously crooked, giving the rug a lopsided look, then no matter how finely detailed it is, drop the rug down two value points.

TABLE 3

Design Description	Value Points
Minutely detailed, small, curvilinear pattern differently detailed throughout the design, which may be either abstract or representational. Almost all of the background is covered by design.	10
Minutely detailed rectilinear designs that cover almost all of the background. Or finely detailed curvilinear allover, medallion, representational, abstract or floral designs.	8
Realistically drawn portrait, figural or picture rugs, or moderately detailed curvilinear, medallion, representational, abstract or floral designs.	7
Moderately detailed curvilinear prayer arch and vase designs (these patterns tend to leave a lot of plain background). Or well-drawn, curvilinear allover designs. Or moderately detailed rectilinear, representational or abstract designs.	6
Less detailed and elaborate designs (such as Heriz-Serapi, as most Heriz are called in the United States). Or medallion designs with plain, open field (e.g., Kirmans).	4
Simple geometric designs (such as typical Afghans). Or elaborately detailed hand-embossed patterned rugs (such as modern Chinese). Or top-grade, thick, heavy Indian rugs of the Aubusson or Savonnerie design with very little background left undecorated.	3
Simple, carved (hand-embossed) designs.	1
Any plain rug.	0

Factor 4: Color

In the following descriptions, I have used the term "color tone" rather than just color. In this way, different shades (grass green or pistachio green, for example) and different tones (dark or light) count as different color tones. White, grey, beige and black also count as color tones.

To evaluate this factor, select the description from Table 4 that best fits the rug and record the appropriate value points. You may have to judge between two descriptions to obtain the proper number.

T A B L E 4

Color Description	Value Points
Nine or more distinct color tones, blended so that no single color jumps out. Rug should use colors in combinations that seem unlikely to work, yet do so amazingly well. Colors may have "jewel" effect, convey a subtle overall glow or have the quality of color used in French Impressionist paintings	10
Seven or more color tones in perfect harmony but lacking the breathtakingly beautiful effect necessary for grade 10. Enough subtlety in the combined use of the various colors so that you have the feeling you would never tire of enjoying them.	8
Five or more color tones that blend well so that no single color jumps out. Rug may have darkly rich effect, be a pretty pastel or be a rainbow of colors, so long as none of the colors are muddied, washed-out or crude. Most modern silk-washed, multicolored Chinese rugs would fit this score. (The single exception would be if the rug is an antique Chinese. In this case, regardless of the *number* of colors, the lowest score I would suggest is 5 and the great majority of the rugs merit a 6.) Only the very best of the thick, heavy type of Indian pieces would qualify.	6
Four or more well-balanced colors such as you might find in rugs from the Turkoman region. Most commercial Kirmans would fit this score, as well as Hamadans and Anatolians.	4

TABLE 4—*Continued*

Color Description	Value Points
Four or more color tones that are prettily blended— except for the addition of crude or "electric" colors which appear to jump out. (Most thick, heavy Indian rugs have at least one crude color.) Or two beautifully rich colors such as you might find in a deep ruby-colored Afghan with its design in midnight blue.	2
Three or more harsh, dreary or muddy color tones. Bleached colors that are faded and patchy. Serious color run. Or a rug which would otherwise fit the "6" description except that the colors have noticeably run into one another.	1
A rug with any number of crude or electric colors that clash unpleasantly. For example, you will find an occasional awful Persian Shiraz or Pakistani rug woven in fire-engine red with violent yellow, pinkish-purple and rich rust. (If such a rug also contained black, brown and white—as would probably be the case—its color *count* would be 7; nevertheless, its color *score* would still be 0.) Any rug woven in only one solid color, e.g., a plain white Indian rug or self-embossed Chinese rug, would, no matter how beautiful the single color, score 0 for the purposes of this table.	0

Factor 5: Age

To determine the number of value points for the age of any rug, interpolate using the following table:

TABLE 5

Age	Value Points
100 years and older	10
70 years and older	8
50 years and older	6
30 years and older	4
20 years and older	2
Below 20 years	0

Factor 6: Condition

To evaluate this factor, select the description that best fits the condition of the rug and record the point value. You may have to judge between descriptions to obtain the correct value.

TABLE 6

Condition Description	Value points
Perfect! No holes, worn spots, stains, patches or traceable repairs of any kind. Pile length should be "as new." Fringes and borders are all present and correct and rug is clean. This description fits most new rugs. (If you find a genuinely old or antique piece the condition of which fits this description, it is a very rare find indeed.)	10
Fringes are loose but not missing and need "stopping." All else is perfect.	9
Excellent except for a repair or two, professionally rewoven, invisible from front and almost invisible from back. Or the pile has been worn down so that it is short (⅛ inch or 3.1 mm. high), but it has been *evenly* worn so that surface of rug is uniform.	8
Apparently excellent condition except that rug is very dirty. No stains have penetrated through to the back of the rug (if they have, they may be impossible to remove). Until the dirt is removed, you can never be sure what you may find underneath. (The rug is unlikely to graduate to a "10" as it probably suffered misuse from whoever allowed it to get so dirty. It might turn out to be an "8" or drop to a "2" if large bald areas appear or stubborn stains remain after cleaning.) If in doubt, drop it down a point or two.	7
Good condition except that you can tell from the symmetry of pattern that some of the borders have been removed or that the rug has had major repair work, not obvious from the front but immediately visible from the back. Or a rug with a hole of about an inch (2.54 cm.) that looks easy to mend.	6
Pile is less than ⅛ inch (3.1 mm.) but some wool remains. Wear is more or less even over full surface	4

TABLE 6—*Continued*

Condition Description	Value Points
and design is clear. Rug should be free of serious stains.	
Moderately stained rug, otherwise in excellent condition. Or pile completely worn away but knots themselves remain, so design is clear. (It could still look beautiful hung on a wall.)	3
Three or four serious cuts several inches long, provided edges of cuts still have knots attached so they can be sewn neatly together. Or fringe has unraveled so part of the rug itself unraveled and was lost. This rating is for rugs that have lost three inches (8 cm.) or more, not just a few rows (half an inch or so). Permanently, noticeably stained rugs.	2
Majority of pattern worn away. A rug that is cracking (see Chapter 7). A rug in worse condition than any of the above. A rug most of which is missing.	0

NOTE: A score of 0 for condition nullifies all other factor value points. One exception is a large rug that can be cut down to exclude the damaged areas and still maintain its beauty.

When you have calculated the value points for the six factors, record them on the chart below. This is column 1. Multiply this number by the number in column 2. Enter the product in column 3. Put the sum of column 3 in the box marked "Total." With this figure you have a way of comparing the approximate *quality* of rugs. (Remember: zero times any number is still zero.)

	1. Value Points	2. Multiplier	3. Product
Knots		12	
Material		7	
Design		6	
Colors		6	
Age		3	
Condition		2	
		TOTAL:	

PRICING A RUG

By far the most critical element in pricing a rug is its country of origin, where it was made. This element involves a combination of prestige, rarity, scarcity, history, future production and market demand. All these things affect the resale value which, in turn, has a direct influence on the investment potential.

To determine the approximate retail price per square foot of a rug, use Table 7 below. Take the figure you computed earlier (in the box labeled "Total") and multiply it by the appropriate number in Table 7. Remember to use the country in which the rug was *made*, not where the design came from. Also, bear in mind that there tends to be a reduction in the price per square foot of a rug if it is a large one.

TABLE 7

Type of Rug	Multiply Value Points by:
Afghan: wool, with knot count below 289	0.47
Afghan: Persia, wool	0.74
Baluchi: Persia, nomadic, wool	0.31
Bijar: Persia, wool	0.70
Bokhara: Persia, Yomud, wool	0.35
Caucasian: Russia, made before 1900	1.60
Chinese: made before 1900	1.50
Chinese: ⅝-inch pile, 90-line	0.29
Egyptian: wool, made after 1945	0.20
Hamadan: Persia, wool	0.34
Hereke: Turkey, fine, silk	3.70
Heriz: Persia, fine, silk, antique	5.00
Heriz: Persia, wool	0.37
Indian: wool, thick, heavy, modern type	0.21
Indo Heriz: Indian, wool	0.13
Isfahan: Persia, fine, silk or *fine* cotton warp	2.10
Kashan: Persia, wool	1.30
Kashmiri: India, wool, with or without touches of silk	0.50
Kayseri: Turkey, art silk (mercerized cotton)	0.27
Kelim: Persia, cotton	0.17
Kirman: Persia, wool, made after 1945	0.43
Meshed: Persia, wool, knot count below 380 per square inch	0.39
Mongol: made before 1920	1.70
Moroccan: wool, made after 1945	0.25

T A B L E 7—*Continued*

Type of Rug	Multiply Value Points by:
Muhd: Persia, wool	0.39
Nain: Persia, fine, with or without touches of silk, cotton warp	1.50
Pakistani: wool, with or without touches of silk	0.18
Qum: Persia, silk	1.90
Qum: Persia, silk-inlaid, kurk wool	1.30
Qum: Persia, wool, with or without touches of silk	0.80
Romanian: wool, modern	0.24
Russian: wool, modern	0.40
Saruk: Persia, wool, made after 1920	0.63
Sinkiang (Samarkand): Chinese, wool, modern	0.14
Taba-Tabriz: Persia, wool	0.51
Tabriz: Persia, with or without silk inlay, kurk wool	3.00
Tabriz: Persia, wool, made after 1945	0.90
Tibetan: 25 to 55 years old	0.54
Turkey: nomadic, made before 1930	0.80
Yallahmeh: Persia, wool	0.43

The final step in pricing a rug is to multiply the price per square foot by the number of square feet in the rug. To determine the square feet in a rug, multiply the length by the width (do not include the fringes). For example, if your rug is 5½ feet long by 3 feet wide (1.68 × .91 m.) the square footage is 16½ (1.52 sq. m.) If you are measuring in inches, multiply the length in inches by the width in inches and divide by 144. This will give you the square footage of the rug. (To calculate square meters from feet, divide square feet by 10.76.)

The price you have calculated includes the retailer's profit. However, it doesn't mean you shouldn't negotiate a lower price as explained in Chapter 8. (The prices being discussed so far are 1985 prices. Later on, I will give you a method for estimating prices for future years.)

If the price you calculate for a rug is significantly *lower* than the merchant's quoted price, one of the following things may be happening:

1. Your value points may be too low. Check them again.
2. You used the wrong multiplier in Table 7. Check again.
3. You miscalculated the square footage in the rug. Check again.
4. The merchant is asking a high price. You can probably get the rug somewhere else for less money.

5. The type and country of rug used in Table 7 is not the right one. Check again with the merchant on name and country of origin.

If the price you calculated for the rug is significantly *higher* than the merchant's quoted price, there could be several reasons:

1. Your value points may be too high. Check them again.
2. You used the wrong multiplier in Table 7. Check again.
3. You miscalculated the square footage of the rug. Check again.
4. The rug is old stock and the merchant hasn't upgraded the price to its present market value—a bargain as compared with present prices.
5. The merchant needs cash and has reduced his profit margin to stimulate turnover—a true bargain, but don't forget to bargain some more. The merchant will still be making a profit and there's no reason you shouldn't share it.
6. The type and country of rug used in Table 7 is not the right one. Check again.

An example of how this can happen would be that the rug in question was made in Meshed, Iran. The merchant refers to it as an Isfahan. So you use the 2.1 multiplier from Table 7 (for the Isfahan) instead of .39 (for the Meshed). This will cause the price to be higher than it should be and you will think you are getting a bargain. If the merchant admits the rug is an Isfahan-Meshed *made* in Meshed, a recalculation will probably show that the "bargain" is no bargain at all. In this example, the merchant may not be lying but simply be caught in a situation that began over twenty years ago. It came about because of a scarcity of *true* Isfahans in the wholesale New York market. The situation became acute in the 1950s and early 1960s. To overcome the problem of practically zero supply and a constant demand, retailers throughout the country began calling rugs from the east Persian town of Meshed and its nearby villages "Isfahan." Even the honest dealers were forced to use the term Isfahan-Meshed or Isfahan-Turkibaff in self-defense. The other dealers were constantly offering "Isfahans" for sale at seemingly low, low prices. These Turkibaffs, as we call them in the trade, have a coarse weave, are thick and cumbersome and are almost always room-sized rugs, twelve by nine feet (3.66 × 2.74 m.) or more. They are also a fraction of the price of a genuine Isfahan. So if you are looking for an Isfahan to invest in, always remember to check its credentials.

SUMMARY

The following examples illustrate the concepts covered so far in this chapter:

EXAMPLE A: This is a fine new Persian silk Qum hanging on the wall in a friend's home. It is seven by four and a half feet (2.13 × 1.37 m.) and has a Persian garden design. I have rated the six factors as follows: knots 7, material 10, design 9, color 8, age 0 and condition 10. This results in a total of 276 value points. In Table 7 I find that the multiplier for silk Qums is 1.9. By multiplying 276 value points by 1.9, I get $524.40 per square foot. Since there are thirty-one and a half square feet in the rug, the retail value of the rug comes out to $16,519.

EXAMPLE B: This is a good classic, new Afghan. It is twelve by nine feet (3.66 × 2.74 m.), thick and heavy, woven on a cotton warp. The background is dark red and the large octagonal designs are dark blue. I have rated the six factors as: knots 3, material 5, design 3, color 2, age 0, condition 10. This makes a total of 121 value points. In Table 7 I find that the multiplier for Afghans is .47. By multiplying 121 value points by .47, I get $56.87 per square foot. Since there are 108 square feet in the rug, the retail value comes to $6,142 for the piece.

EXAMPLE C: This is an above-average new Pakistani rug. It is five by three feet, four inches (1.52 × 1.02 m.), regular in shape, has glossy wool, a well-executed design and a variety of colors. I have rated the six factors as follows: knots 6, material 5, design 5, color 6, age 0, condition 10. This results in a total of 193 value points. In Table 7 I find that the multiplier for Pakistani rugs is .18. By multiplying the value points 193 by .18, I get $34.74 per square foot. Because there are sixteen and two-thirds square feet in the piece, the retail value is $579.

EXAMPLE D: This is an average-to-good, wool heavy new Indian rug. It is twelve by nine feet (3.66 × 2.74 m.), has thick pile, four colors, is hand-embossed with few design features. I have rated the six factors as follows: knots 2, material 2, design 1, color 2, age 0 and condition 10. This comes to a total of 76 value points. The multiplier in Table 7 for Indian rugs is .21. By multiplying the 76 value points by .21, I get $15.96 per square foot. Since there are 108 square feet in the rug, the retail value for this piece comes out to $1,724.

Table 8 below is a listing of forty actual rugs that I have

examined and rated for your ready reference. Remember, *the rugs you are evaluating are different from the ones on this list.* Even so, this list will give you some relative values and reference points for a quick check.

TABLE 8

Type of Rug	Value Points	Multiplier	1985 Price per Sq. Ft. U.S. $
Afghan: wool, cotton warp, new	121	0.47	56.87
Afshar: Persia, wool, cotton warp, new	160	0.24	38.40
Baluchi: Persia, nomadic, 25 years old	187	0.31	57.97
Bijar: Persia, wool, new	205	0.70	143.50
Bokhara: Persia, Yomud, wool, new	145	0.35	50.75
Caucasian: Russia, Daghestan, before 1850	218	1.60	348.80
Chinese: made before 1900	189	1.50	283.50
Chinese: new, wool (⅝" pile)	127	0.29	36.83
Egyptian: wool, new	133	0.29	38.60
Hamadan: Persia, wool, new	133	0.34	45.22
Hereke: Turkey, fine, silk, new	306	3.70	1,132.20
Heriz: Persia, fine, silk, antique	328	5.00	1,640.00
Heriz: Persia, wool, new	139	0.37	51.43
Indian: new, thick, heavy, wool, Aubusson design	76	0.21	15.96
Indo Heriz: Indian, wool, new	112	0.13	14.56
Isfahan: Persia, fine, silk warp, new	281	2.10	590.10
Kashan: Persia, new, wool	212	1.30	275.60
Kashmiri: India, new, silk-inlaid	194	0.50	97.00
Kayseri: Turkey, art silk (mercerized cotton)	149	0.27	40.23
Kelim: Persia, cotton, new	113	0.17	19.21
Kirman: Persia, wool, new	151	0.43	64.93
Meshed: Persia, wool, new	163	0.39	63.57
Mongolian: made before 1920	189	1.70	321.30
Moroccan: wool, new	62	0.25	15.50
Muhd: Persia, wool, new	187	0.39	72.93
Nain: Persia, touches of silk, new	275	1.50	412.50
Pakistani: Bokhara design, wool, new	193	0.18	34.74
Qum: Persia, new, silk	276	1.90	524.40

TABLE 8—*Continued*

Type of Rug	Value Points	Multiplier	1985 Price per Sq. Ft. U.S. $
Qum: Persia, new, silk-inlaid, kurk wool	263	1.30	341.90
Qum: Persia, small touches of silk inlay, wool, new	194	0.80	155.20
Romanian: wool, medium quality	151	0.24	36.24
Russian: Bokhara design, wool, new	181	0.40	72.40
Saruk: Persia, rose background, floral, wool, made about 1940	214	0.63	134.82
Sinkiang (Samarkand): Chinese, wool, new	145	0.14	20.30
Taba-Tabriz: Persia, wool, new	169	0.51	86.19
Tabriz: Persia, silk-inlaid, kurk wool, new	281	3.00	843.00
Tabriz: Persia, good wool, new	205	0.90	184.50
Tibetan: made about 1955	128	0.54	69.12
Turkey: nomadic, made about 1930	175	0.80	140.00
Yallahmeh: Persia, wool, new	175	0.43	75.25

Table 9 is a list of value points for many of the rugs you are likely to encounter. This table will prove useful as a check against your value-point calculations. If you are not within the range, yet you feel your value points are roughly correct, then your rug may not be the type you think it is; e.g., perhaps it was made in Pakistan, not Persia.

Note: I have excluded a 0 score on the condition factor in these ranges as any rug rating a 0 would void all other factors. Therefore, the minimum value point score a rug could receive on condition is 1 in these ranges.

TABLE 9

Type of Rug	Minimum Value Points	Maximum Value Points
Afghan: wool, with knot count below 289	57	212
Afshar: Persia, wool	94	268
Baluchi: Persia, nomadic, wool	90	229
Caucasian: Russia, made before 1900	124	302
Chinese: made before 1900	76	235

T A B L E 9—*Continued*

Type of Rug	Miminum Value Point	Maximum Value Point
Chinese: ⅝-inch pile, 90-line	67	157
Hamadan: Persia, wool	70	236
Hereke: Turkey, fine, silk	216	360*
Heriz: Persia, wool	70	223
Heriz: Persia, fine, silk, antique	270	336
Indian: wool, thick, heavy, modern type	21	145
Isfahan: Persia, fine, silk or *fine* cotton warp	182	347*
Kashan: Persia, wool	130	290
Kashmiri: India, wool, with or without silk inlay	100	277
Kayseri: Turkey, art silk (mercerized cotton)	95	197
Kirman: Persia, wool, made after 1945	100	218
Meshed: Persia, wool, with knot count below 380 per square inch	88	229
Pakistani: wool, with or without touches of silk	82	217
Qum: Persia, silk	192	306
Qum: Persia, silk-inlaid, kurk wool, on silk or *fine* cotton warp	233	293
Qum: Persia, wool, with or without touches of silk	100	242
Romanian: wool, modern	121	229
Saruk: Persia, wool, made after 1920	100	223
Sinkiang (Samarkand): Chinese, wool	89	205
Tabriz: Persia, wool, made after 1945	82	292

* 330 if new.

A word of caution: I have been discussing 1985 estimated retail prices in this chapter. Because prices are in a state of constant change, I can give you only a snapshot as I see it at the present time. A country's political situation and its effect on rug production and exports can change overnight, as we experienced with Iran (Persia) in 1979 and Afghanistan in 1980. The socio-economic change in an area can affect rug prices and availability, although this is usually more gradual. And, of course, there is the United States Customs, which can increase or decrease the duty on rugs, thus affecting prices virtually overnight. Nevertheless, I feel it is worthwhile to give you some idea of relative prices. As mentioned earlier, one of the best ways to avoid being cheated is to deal with a reputable company. But it is reassuring to have a way of checking for oneself.

PROJECTING PRICES INTO THE FUTURE

Attempting to predict prices of rugs involves two elements. The first is an analysis of price movement in the recent past. Here we are dealing with facts and figures which are readily available. The second comes under the heading of crystal-gazing. Here we are trying to guess—by country—such tricky factors as inflation, market demand, political upheavals and socio-economic trends. By combining these two elements, we can arrive at some rough predictions of future prices.

I have pored over thousands of rug prices for the years since 1969 and have asked knowledgeable people hundreds of questions about the future. I have concluded that rugs can be grouped in three categories, whose values will probably increase at rates of (1) 25% per year or more, (2) 15% to 20% per year, and (3) 5% to 10% per year.

Category 1: Rugs going up in value
at a rate of 25% per year or more

This category contains ten old, good rugs and six top-quality new ones. Some of these will increase in value more than others, but it is conservatively estimated that they all will increase at a rate of 25% per year.

Caucasian, old	Mongol, old
Chinese, old	Nain
Kashan, old	Persian, old, nomadic (i.e., Baluchi)
Heriz, old, silk	Qum, silk
Isfahan, new	Qum, kurk wool, with or
Isfahan, old	without silk inlay

Saruk, old	Tibetan, old
Tabriz, kurk wool, silk-inlaid	Turkish, old, nomadic
Tabriz, good wool	

The following table shows a rug worth $1,000 in 1985 increasing at a rate of 25% per year:

Year	Price	Year	Price
1986	$1,250	1991	$3,815
1987	1,563	1992	4,768
1988	1,953	1993	5,960
1989	2,441	1994	7,451
1990	3,052	1995	9,314

Thus, assuming that the annual rate of increase continues at 25%, in ten years, a rug in this category would be worth nine times its present price, a return on investment of 831%.

Category 2: Rugs going up in value at a rate of 15% to 20% per year

This category is divided into two sections. The first contains ten rugs going up in value at about 20% per year, the second contains ten rugs going up at about 15% per year.

20%	*15%*
Afshar	Afghan, new wool
Baluchi	Greek
Bijar	Kashmiri, wool
Hamadan	Kayseri
Heriz	Kelim, Persia
Kirman	Kashmiri, silk-inlaid
Muhd	Meshed
Qum, wool with or	Russian
without silk inlay	Sinkiang (Samarkand)
Taba-Tabriz	Yomud Bokhara
Yallahmeh	

The following table shows a $1,000 rug in 1985 increasing at rates of 20% and 15% per year:

Year	Price at 20%	Price at 15%
1986	$1,200	$1,150
1987	1,440	1,323
1988	1,728	1,521
1989	2,074	1,749
1990	2,488	2,011
1991	2,986	2,313
1992	3,583	2,660
1993	4,300	3,059
1994	5,160	3,518
1995	6,192	4,046

Thus, in ten years, a rug increasing in value at 20% per year would be worth 6 times as much, a 520% return on investment; one growing at 15% would be worth 4 times as much, a 305% return.

Category 3: Rugs going up in value at a rate of 5% to 10% per year

This category is divided into two sections. The first contains five rugs going up in value at about 10% per year; the second contains four rugs hardly keeping up with inflation by increasing at about 5% per year.

10%	5%
Agra	Chinese, all other modern
Chinese (⅝-inch pile, 90-line)	Indian
Egyptian	Moroccan
Pakistani	Sinkiang (Samarkand)
Romanian	

The following table shows a $1,000 rug in 1985 increasing at rates of 10% and 5% per year:

Year	Price at 10%	Price at 5%
1986	$1,100	$1,050
1987	1,210	1,102
1988	1,331	1,158
1989	1,464	1,215
1990	1,611	1,276
1991	1,772	1,340
1992	1,949	1,407

Year	Price at 10%	Price at 5%
1993	2,144	1,477
1994	2,358	1,551
1995	2,594	1,629

Thus, in ten years a rug increasing in value at 10% per year would be worth 2.6 times its present value, a return on investment of 160%; one growing at 5% would be worth only 1.6 times, a 60% return.

Remember, inflation will account for a portion of the ten-year price increase. However, the genuine growth (subtracting inflation) is still impressive, especially with Category One rugs. This growth trend is not new but has been going on for generations. For example, in 1939, a new Isfahan sold for $1 per square foot retail, as compared with $590 today!

It is also interesting to compare the growth of rugs with other well-known investment articles. In the period June 1969 to June 1979, rough diamonds, Old Master paintings and rare United States coins increased about 12% annually, while stamps and gold increased about 20% annually. Old Baluchis, on the other hand, increased an average of 35% per year over the same period. I will be giving you a list of my personal favorite "investor's rugs" later in this chapter.

How to Determine a Rug's Value in the Years Ahead

Step 1. With a specific rug in mind, calculate its 1982 value as explained earlier in this chapter.

Step 2. Determine whether the rug falls into Category One, Two or Three and note the appropriate percentage to be used.

Step 3. Add 100% to the percent figure determined in Step 2 (e.g., 100% + 20% = 120%).

Step 4. Chart the rug's value growth as follows:

Value in 1985 = $_____ (insert answer to Step 1 here)

Value in 1986 = $_____ (the 1985 figure multiplied by the percentage determined in Step 3)

Value in 1987 = $_____ (the 1986 figure multiplied by the percentage determined in Step 3)

Value in 1988 = $_____ (the 1987 figure multiplied by the percentage determined in Step 3)

And so on.

You will recall the four examples used in calculating 1985 rug prices. The first was a silk Qum, the second an Afghan, the third a Pakistani and the last an Indian. Using the above procedure, the 1988 values for these particular rugs are estimated as follows:

Example	1985 Value	1988 Value
A: the silk Qum (7' × 4'6")	$16,519	$32,264
B: the Afghan (12' × 9')	$ 6,142	$ 9,341
C: the Pakistani (5' × 3'4")	$ 579	$ 771
D: the Indian (12' × 9')	$ 1,724	$ 1,996

You now have a way of evaluating rugs you already own; estimating the price of a rug you contemplate buying now; and projecting the value of your rugs for the future.

BUYING FOR INVESTMENT

There are few things in this world that have consistently increased in value throughout the decades as much as oriental rugs. The key is to select good specimens, as they command top prices. If you are not knowledgeable, I would strongly recommend you obtain expert advice. A reputable dealer or broker could prove very useful. They are professional, experienced people who have the necessary contacts. If you have doubts about the selection or the price, get a trustworthy, unbiased second opinion. Remember, it is extremely rare that one gets a real bargain from the stranger coming to your door with a rug under his arm, or at an auction or a sale in a department store. Investors make their money by selecting rugs that will increase the most in the years ahead. They are willing to sacrifice the broker's fee for the best growth rate.

The following is a list of rugs I would recommend for investment and the reasons why. You will note that they are not all at the high end of the price range. However, I believe they will increase sixfold in six years.

OLDER KASHAN RUGS: There are two main reasons why I am predicting that the price of the "older" Kashans (30 years old or more) will continue to rise impressively. The first is that the demand for these classic, glowing rugs exceeds the supply both in the West and in the Middle East, where fine Kashans are regarded as thoroughly sound investments. Second, Kashans are now sought after by those top-ranking U.S. interior designers who regularly set the style for the rest of the fashion-conscious world.

QUM RUGS *(especially fine silk ones):* The city of Qum is regarded by the Iranians as a holy city. Many of its deeply religious people disapprove of the lighter things in life. Even the city's only cinema was deliberately burned down. It is said that this was done "so that the faithful would not have the distraction of frivolous entertainment." The extravagant luxury of Qum's silken rugs is the antithesis of this attitude. Today the weavers in Qum seem to be producing only commercial rugs. These are rather casually woven from medium and even poor grades of silk. However, in the free markets of both Europe and the United States, it is still possible to find silk Qums of true investment quality. These are well worth searching for, but only consider rugs woven before 1980; very few good Qums have been produced since then. The good ones are easy to spot: Their silk is lustrous, their weave is dense, their designs are always well defined, and their colors have a wonderful jewel-like quality.

ISFAHAN RUGS: The development of Iran's national oil industry is causing major changes in the life-style of the people of Isfahan. Besides which, the shock waves of recent political upheavals in Iran were particularly severe in Isfahan. It is becoming more and more difficult to find good examples of the incredibly fine rugs that are woven in and around this beautiful city. The prices of those rugs that are available are soaring. (See page 192.)

NAIN RUGS: The village of Nain, being close to Isfahan, is strongly influenced by the events there. Nain's old, peaceful way of life has been disrupted and few of the villagers are spending their time weaving the very fine rugs any more. The Middle Eastern

Camels are very much a part of a nomad's life. They provide milk, meat, and transportation; also, their hair can be used in weaving rugs.

buyers, and in particular the Iranians themselves, have long considered Nains to be one of the best types of Persian rugs.

ALL NOMADIC RUGS *(especially Baluchis):* In this case I would definitely suggest your buying the older pieces, although any nomadic rug, whether it is old or new, that has a good design, rich coloring and a knot count above 120 per square inch is worth considering.

Times are hard for the nomads, and in particular for the Baluchis. The new governing authorities of both Iran and Afghanistan prefer the nomads to settle in stable communities and so the nomadic way of life has virtually come to an end. This type of rug, together with all the other nomadic rugs, is, in my opinion, very underpriced at the moment. The rugs of those Baluchis who settled on the outskirts of Meshed are attractive and well made but they are different—for me, they lack the spontaneity of the true nomadic pieces.

TABRIZ RUGS: The price of the *fine* Tabriz rugs is rising as this town in northwestern Iran becomes more and more industrialized. I believe that, although the commercial type of Tabriz rugs will continue to be available for some years, the "investment quality" finely woven Tabriz rugs are now uneconomical to produce. You can still find good examples in the stores today, but I doubt that they will be available tomorrow.

OLD CHINESE, MONGOL AND TIBETAN RUGS: The style of weaving in China drastically changed in the early part of this century. The thick, modern, deeply embossed rugs and carpets that China now produces bear little resemblance to the lovely old and antique pieces with their restrained color schemes and meaningful designs. This is why I am recommending the old Chinese rugs as being investment pieces, along with the old Tibetan and Mongol ones. Few if any rugs are now being exported from Mongolia and since the Chinese invasion of Tibet, the new Tibetan rugs are adulterated versions of the old ones. There is a growing appreciation for all three of these types of old rugs by the West and the supply is running out.

A yard on the edge of the bazaar in Kashan. The "white" Kashan carpet in the foreground has a Shah Abbas design and is a typical example of a good modern Kashan.

CHAPTER TEN

The Rug Bug

For many Middle Eastern peoples and Iranians in particular, oriental rugs are the equivalent of our stocks and shares and will form a major part of their estate. A rich Persian household, for example, may have a hundred fine rugs piled one on top of the other, securely locked up in a private room in their home or in the vaults of the local bank. Even the relatively poor nomad or villager will have a few precious pieces tucked away.

Whether or not you intend to collect rugs as an investment, collecting them should be fun—especially now that you have almost finished reading this book and have the necessary guidelines to help you avoid making costly mistakes. There are four basic points to consider before you begin your collection: the first of these is knowing what you want; the second is money; the third is the amount of space you have to house your rugs; and the fourth is knowing where to *buy* your rug and, should you change your mind, where to *sell* it. This fourth point needs some further discussion.

BUYING AND SELLING RUGS

Throughout this book I have encouraged you to find and build up a relationship with a reputable, reliable rug supplier. This is especially important if you are considering getting more than one rug in the years to come. Whether you choose to buy through an interior designer, from a retail oriental rug store or through the trade via a broker will probably depend on three things: the price you are willing to pay; the inconvenience you are willing to put up with; and the extent of involvement you want in the selection of your rugs. Whichever way you choose, my advice is that you spend some time in finding a supplier you both like and trust. Then you will always feel comfortable if you need to ask for their help or advice in the future. Rugs are very individual items and a supplier who takes a personal interest in your collection can be invaluable. Just one of the advantages is that they will probably keep records on file of your collection and so may be able to give you updated evaluations of your rugs without necessarily having to see them.

Buying your rugs through an interior designer is probably the most convenient method, although perhaps not the most inexpensive. Designers are frequently asked to include oriental rugs in their overall schemes. Consequently, they are usually familiar with at least two or three wholesalers who can provide advice and a wide variety of the types of oriental rugs that designers like to use. The designers rarely claim to have an expert knowledge of rugs, but the good ones do have an intuitive understanding of the colorings and designs of rugs and they are able to utilize their talent to highlight a rug's beauty. Because the floor is literally the foundation for the whole atmosphere of the room, many designers feel that the rug is the number one item to be determined. (Once a floor's covering is selected, it can be both expensive and difficult to alter.) When they are using orientals, designers will either search through dozens of rugs on your behalf, narrowing the field to a few ideal pieces from which you can then select; or they will make the final choice for you and all you have to do is pay the bill.

As a general rule, interior designers earn their fees on the difference between the trade price and the retail price. Naturally, fees are a private matter between the client and the designer, and many designers will not accept assignments where less than $60,000 is to be spent on the project. However, there are some budget designers who are prepared to take on projects of a more modest $5,000–$6,000 range. These can be contacted via the American Society of Interior Designers (730 Fifth Avenue, New York, N.Y. 10019; 212-586-7111), which runs a free referral service in the New York metropolitan area.

If you decide to buy a rug on your own through a specialist rug store, do try to choose a store that has been established long enough to have gained a good reputation. Their reputation is likely to be much more important to them than a quick profit. (Ask your friends where they bought their rugs. This can be especially helpful if they own two or three.) A store that has been in business for several years can not only be relied upon to advise you on the type of rug most suitable to your needs, but they will have built up enough stock over the years to offer you a proper selection from which to choose. The prices of the rugs should always be clearly marked, either on their tags or on a list which you are allowed to look at.

Specialist rug stores can also help you to *sell* your rug if you decide that it is no longer suitable. In my opinion, this is one of the safest and most satisfactory ways of selling rugs, provided that you know that the store is trustworthy. Arrange to take your rug to the store so that either the owner or the manager can advise you as to how much they feel the rug is worth. *Before* they suggest a price, do make it clear that you do not want them to buy your rug outright but rather to sell it in their store on your behalf. This should help to ensure that the price they quote is the retail one (the tag price). Don't be surprised if they also tactfully suggest that you both agree to set a minimum selling price at the same time (this will allow the store owners a bargaining range when they, in turn, sell the rug). So long as the gap between the two prices is no more than 10 percent of the total price, you shouldn't let this bother you. After all, you want your rug to be competitive with others in the store, and, as I've discussed in Chapter 9, there are circumstances where the retailer needs maneuverability in order to make a sale.

Once your rug has been sold, the store will then deduct their previously agreed selling percentage (usually about 25 percent) before sending you the balance of the money. Short of opening your own rug store, I believe that this is the best way of getting the best price, with a minimum risk. However, selling your rug in this way can take a long time. If your rug is an unusual size or color, or if it is very expensive, you may have to wait many months before it finds a new home. Meanwhile, when you visit your rug, you have the reassurance of knowing that it is being properly looked after and insured while it is on display. After a few weeks, if you change your mind (provided, of course, that the rug is still unsold), you can always take it home again.

If you are buying your rug in a department store, it is essential that you make certain that the salesperson is knowledgeable about rugs. No matter how pleasant a person may be, if that person's regular job is in the lampshade department, he or she is unlikely to be able to give you the expert advice you need. So always try to get the help of the buyer for the rug department or of a senior salesperson who really understands oriental rugs.

Buying your oriental rug through the trade from an established, reliable broker can save you money—lots of it. Brokers do not have to worry about the expenses of running a smart store, or the costs of stocking a large number of rugs which then take months and in some cases years to sell. A broker's task is to buy the best and most suitable rugs available on the market for clients, at the time when the clients are ready to buy. So brokers only charge a small buying commission, which is normally added on to the wholesale merchant's price. The choice of rugs that a good broker can offer you is virtually unlimited. You can almost dream up a rug, old or new, and ask the broker to find it!

By employing a broker as you go through all the various warehouses, you will have someone with you to look after your interests. Because the kind of brokers that I am describing are independent, they can take you to whichever wholesalers are offering, at that time, the most suitable rugs at the most competitive prices. If brokers feel that the price of any individual rug is too high, they are free to tell you. If the quality of the rug bothers them, they can tell you. They also look after details, such as getting the rug you choose shipped or delivered to your home.

The snags in buying through a broker are that you have to tramp around drafty, dusty warehouses, standing patiently while piles of rugs are turned over for your inspection, and after all that you won't have the convenience of being able to try out the rugs in your own home. The wholesalers seldom allow their rugs out on approval; it complicates their paperwork and may also involve paying a customs duty. Rugs are often held in the warehouses under a customs and excise bond so they can avoid incurring local importation duties if the wholesale merchant sells them for use overseas.

Buying your rug through a broker can be fun but it can also be very tiring. You may even have to make two or three visits to the warehouses before you find your ideal rug in the stack. Finding a good broker also takes time, and a little luck. The best way of finding one is by way of recommendation. Rug brokers may also help you if you want to sell your rug, but because they are dealing at trade price levels, you're not likely to make as much money as you would by selling it through a retail store or at auction.

If you have been interested in oriental rugs for any length of time, you will probably have read articles warning all but the most dedicated experts to stay away from rug auctions. Personally, I think this is a shame. Auctions can be very interesting so long as you are fully conscious of the possible pitfalls and remember the phrase: Buyer take care.

As a general rule, auctions fall into two categories. Category One includes all the honest, highly respectable auction houses, both large and small, which are run by responsible auctioneers; I see no reason why you should not feel free to enjoy these auctions. Category Two covers those other, often widely advertised, disreputable auctions. These are frequently located in motels and hotels throughout the country. Category Two rug auctions are organized by a few companies whose objective seems to be making money out of the general public's lack of knowledge about rugs. If you suspect an auction you are attending falls into this category, my advice is to leave as quickly as you can.

One way of deciding which category a particular auction falls into is to use much the same criteria as I have suggested you use to choose a retail store: Find out whether or not the auction house is an established company with a good reputation. Do they sell other things besides rugs? If so, this is a good sign. Category Two auctions almost always deal *only* in rugs. If the company holds regular auctions, try to discover whether they will sell rugs *for* you as well as *to* you. Also do check to see if they have a proper office to which you could take any complaints.

Noticing how much time has been allowed to preview the rugs is helpful. Category One auction houses always try to allow a preview of at least a whole day, often two days, so that people can really see and examine the things they want to bid for. Ask how long the auction itself is expected to last. If the answer is "about two hours," check your catalogue. If you see that there are two hundred rugs listed for sale, you may well wonder just how they intend to auction off each rug in thirty-six seconds flat. What this sort of puzzle is possibly indicating is that the company actually has no intention of auctioning all the rugs. In these cases, the procedure usually is for cheap, poor-quality rugs to be auctioned first (often contrary to the order of the catalogue); or else, for a couple of fine-quality, obviously expensive rugs to be "bought" by members of the auctioneer's staff to encourage the public to bid. Then, about an hour after the auction has begun, the auctioneer complains, saying that the sale is badly attended or that the level of bidding is appallingly low, using phrases such as "These rugs are too precious to hand out at give-away prices." The auctioneer might then go on to say that because the company has received instructions that the rugs must be sold as soon as possible, those who are seriously interested in buying may make their offers privately after the auction is over. The impression given is that if you stay behind, you may be able to get this or that beautiful rug (carefully displayed under the spotlights) for a fraction of what it would have cost you if it had actually been auctioned. In fact, you would probably find yourself surrounded by the company's highly skilled salespeople, asking three times as much as the rugs are worth and finally agreeing to sell them to you for twice as much as they are worth. They would need only a few successful sales like this to pay all the expenses of setting up the auction: hiring of the room, advertising, porters' wages, plus providing the members of the team with a handsome profit.

The catalogue can provide you with another hint as to the validity of the auction. Look for prefixes such as "Kaba," which means "coarse." For example, a "Kaba Prayer rug woven from art silk in Anatolia" just means a coarse prayer rug made from mercerized cotton in Turkey. "Haroun" can also mean "coarse" or "poor quality." Haroun is the name of a village within the area of the Persian town of Kashan and the rugs produced there do look like proper Kashans, but Harouns are of much lower quality. The term "Mori" is also often misleadingly used. Mori is a town in Afghanistan where excellent hard-wearing, expensive, Bokhara-design rugs are made. However, "Mori Bokhara" has come to mean any Bokhara-design rug made in *Pakistan.* Category One auctioneers will say so; Category Two auctioneers won't.

On the other hand, it is also true that some prefixes can be very positive. For instance, "inely" means "good." "Kurk" refers to top-quality wool and "gulestan" just means "rose garden." (Good Ushak rugs are often called Gulestan Ushaks.) It is a matter of adding up all the various hints and using your own judgment as to which kind of auction is being held. Prefixes can be fun and important to collect.

It is worth noting that "warehouse sales" and "fire-damaged rugs" may indicate Category Two type activities. For instance, this is one way of disposing of rugs that the trade people have refused to buy. Also, sales advertised as "canceled export orders" may be suspect. Just because a sale is being held near an airport doesn't necessarily mean that the rugs were booked to go anywhere.

If you are attending a straightforward Category One auction, the only real risk is that in the excitement of the sale, people sometimes find themselves bidding much higher than they had originally intended. I shall always remember the first auction I went to many years ago which was held in the small town of Banbury in England. It was wintertime and the cottage I was living in was cold. At the auction the electric heater sitting in an old cardboard carton together with a hot-water bottle seemed just what I needed. The tag on the heater read "Lot No. 12, in good working order." Twelve was my lucky number and I decided to bid up to £3. I got Lot No. 12 (although I ended up bidding £2 over the limit I had set myself) and I felt rather pleased. It was as I was going home that I realized my mistake. There, in the Electricity Boards showroom window, was a shiny new version of my heater priced at £4. (Until that moment, I had considered myself a prudent shopper.)

Nowadays before an auction begins, I make it a golden rule to mark up my catalogue with my highest limit which I never, ever exceed—oriental rugs cost a great deal more money than electric heaters and hot-water bottles.

If you want to auction a rug of your own, different auction companies specialize in different classifications of rugs. It makes little sense to take a fine new rug to a company that specializes in antiques. Even if the auction house accepts your rug, the price it sells it for might be disappointingly low. If you want to sell a rug at auction, selecting the most suitable auction house can make all the difference. Choosing the right time of year is also important. Holiday seasons, when a lot of people are away, is the time to buy—but not to sell. Besides, the way in which your rug is described in the catalogue can make a difference in the price it sells for. For example, a "handmade woolen Persian Kashan rug" will probably sell for more money than if the rug were listed as "an oriental rug."

If you want to buy or sell rugs at auction, the following suggestions may help you avoid making expensive mistakes:

Do avoid Category Two auctions.
Do decide at the preview which rugs you are interested in.
Do *thoroughly* examine each rug all over before you decide to bid for it.
    (Often parts of rugs are inadvertently hidden under furniture; ask for this to be moved aside, or forget the rug.)
Do ask an expert to go with you to the preview if you are thinking of spending a considerable amount of money. The small fees that experts usually charge for this service could save you a lot of anxiety.
Do decide what your highest bid should be before the auction begins, and then stick with it.
Do bid calmly, joining in as the bidding slows down.

Do make sure that the auctioneer notices your bid.
Do go to auctions held when the weather is bad (you may be the only one there).

_____

Don't think that just because you pay $1,000 for a rug you can necessarily auction it the next week and get your $1,000 back. Auction companies have to make money to stay in business so they usually take a commission of around 10 to 15 percent from both the buyer and the seller.
Don't forget that many problem rugs end up at auctions.
Don't forget that "silk" doesn't necessarily mean that it's top-quality silk. (In some circumstances, silk may be used to describe mercerized cotton.)
Don't forget to take this book (Chapter 9) and your pocket calculator with you to the preview to help you calculate how much a rug should cost.
Don't feel you must buy something just because you are there.
Don't forget there are other rugs in the world if someone outbids you.

Placing an advertisement in your local newspaper can be a very simple way of selling a rug. However, if you are offered a check instead of cash, it's wise to be sure to clear it through your bank *before* parting with the rug. Choosing a time of year when the weather is nice is a good idea, too, for if you live in the country you can then show people the rug in your garage and avoid having to invite strangers into your home. Do be prepared for the possibility of unkind remarks being made about your rug. Sometimes, unscrupulous people do this in order to force the price down. This may also happen if you take your rug to a dealer. Many, but by no means all, dealers have a habit of disapproving of any rugs that are brought to them by private individuals. Often this is because they want to sell you a rug of their own.

COLLECTING RUGS

There are any number of ways to plan your collection of oriental rugs. You may want to be eclectic and choose a selection of rugs just because you like them. Or you may decide to build your collection around a theme. You might choose flowers or dragons or animals as your theme. Alternatively you could choose only rugs that include the graceful Arabic script in their designs. Or you may prefer to collect rugs that have been signed by the weaver, or rugs that have been made by the nomadic tribes whose life-style has changed so little over the centuries that they

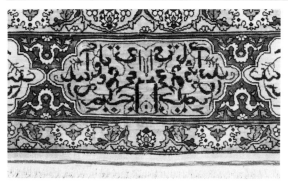

An Arabic script enclosed in a cartouche. Such scripts are often used in border designs of rugs that have religious significance.

still weave saddlebags for their pack animals. Maybe you would like to have all rectilinear or all curvilinear design rugs. Another idea is to collect one basic color. Blue, for instance, could include rugs from the deepest sapphires to the palest powder blues. So long as your rugs share your favorite color, you will find them easy to live with and they should make a unified collection.

Some people collect only rugs that are pure silk. Many of these pieces have one-way designs that are ideal to use as wall hangings. Other people specialize in pictorial rugs that tell stories, such as the Kashan illustrated on page 226. This rug pictures Shah Abbas the Great (top border, center) who is said to have been amused by the sorry tale of Farhad depicted in the body of the rug:

A young sculptor from the provinces, by the name of Farhad, while stopping over at an oasis, fell in love with Shirin, daughter of the Shah. The courageous Farhad fought his way past the palace guard and forced his way directly to the person of the Shah whom he then asked for the hand of his daughter. The Shah agreed on the condition that Farhad carve out a palace for him inside a mountain. Shirin prayed that Farhad would have the strength to accomplish this task quickly. After several years of strenuous work he finally completed the palace. The people were jubilant, and all looked forward to a magnificent wedding of the princess and her beloved Farhad.

Soon thereafter an old woman came to the Shah and asked him if he intended to keep his promise to Farhad. The sovereign replied that he had no other choice, for his word of honour was involved.

The old woman then assured the Shah that if he would give her alms she would free him of his obligation, and no injustice would thereby ensue. It would only be necessary, she said, for all the sheep in the kingdom to be locked up in their stalls for four days. And so it was done. And then, when the animals were freed again on the fifth day, they began to bleat and cry out aloud. A great sound was created which echoed and resounded through the mountains.

A pictorial Kashan rug.

The old woman had arranged it so that she would be near Farhad just at the time when this echo could be heard. The sounds disturbed Farhad considerably, and he asked the old woman what the meaning of all the noise was. She replied that they were cries of anguish because the Princess Shirin had suddenly died. At this, Farhad climbed up on a rocky precipice and threw himself to his death in a gorge deep below.

When Shirin learned of the death of her beloved she went at once to her father and explained that she wanted to view the spot where Farhad had died. Then, accompanied by one of her ladies-in-waiting, she climbed the *very same precipice. Then, when her companion's attention was distracted for an instant, Shirin rushed to the edge and leapt into the chasm below—to join her lover in paradise.*

One of my clients buys only prayer rugs. It doesn't matter whether they are antique or brand new or whether they have been made in Turkey, Afghanistan or Persia—just so long as they are prayer rugs. The client likes these small (typically five by three feet—1.52 × .91 m.) rugs because they can be easily moved to change the moods and colorings of her home.

Another client loves flowering trees, so trees became the theme of her rug collection. Some of her rugs have trees that are tiny and intermingled with animals and flowers surrounding a medallion. Other rugs show the tree-of-life design that has one large flowering tree spreading across the entire rug. She also has marriage-tree rugs (where two trees of life intertwine), garden-of-paradise and forest-design rugs. Because so many different designs include trees, she hasn't found her theme to be at all limiting. When you see the collection the effect is that of a garden, full of color and light and graceful shapes.

Some people use geography as their theme, choosing all their rugs from one small area, town or village. An advantage to having this sort of collection is that you can be sure the pieces will blend together. Although I personally find this idea restricting, it does make it easier to become an expert because you can concentrate on one particular type of rug. You will also quickly become familiar with their prices so that you can avoid unpleasant surprises when you come to buy them. Another advantage is that your rug suppliers may save special pieces for you because they know exactly what you are looking for. If you are a good client and the rugs you specialize in are not unduly expensive, they may even buy a few pieces specifically with you in mind.

I have one client who uses money as his theme: his boast is that all the rugs in his collection cost less than $400. Obviously, with the constantly increasing prices of rugs, his choice is becoming limited. However, he can still buy pieces from Pakistan, India and occasionally from other places as well. He makes a habit of visiting his local auctioneers and when they have a poorly attended sale he sometimes finds a real bargain. He has also left a standing order with my company to buy any attractive pieces, no matter how old or worn-out they may be, just so long as the holes are not too large and the pattern is still traceable. One of his hobbies is to "tint" and repair rugs, as I have described in Chapter 6.

Many investors collect only the finest new pieces and so

avoid paying a premium for antique rugs. They buy rugs that will be the antiques of the future. As I have already discussed, this means that the serious investor usually avoids buying new rugs that have been made in either Pakistan or China. The Chinese in particular are producing far too many rugs, and although they are well made from good materials, they have lost their originality. The old pieces are definitely worth buying (see Chapter 9).

Some rug collections consist of kelims; some of rugs under a certain size, rugs over or under a certain age, rugs with unusual shapes—the variety of themes seems endless. For my own collection I have simply chosen the best rugs I could find within my three basic limits: I really like each one; they did not break the bank; and I did not have to build a new home to accommodate them.

After you have chosen your first rug, don't forget to check your household insurance policy regarding oriental rugs. Rug-jacking is on the increase. To be fully reimbursed for a stolen rug, many policies require a description (a photograph is even better) of the rug and some companies charge a small additional premium. The extra protection is worth the effort; otherwise, you may only be reimbursed for a fraction of your rug's present value. The question to ask your insurance broker is "I own a rug that has a replacement value of $3,000. If only the rug is stolen, will I be reimbursed the $3,000? If not, how much will I receive?" In some instances, the answer may be only a few hundred dollars. If this is the case, it is worthwhile to find out what it would take to obtain full coverage. Sometimes a valuation certificate is all that is required to get full coverage, and this is usually free if you contact the store from which you bought the rug.

CUSTOM-MADE RUGS

Having an oriental rug custom-made may be difficult, but it's not impossible. It does cost rather more than buying a rug "off the loom," but then a custom-tailored suit costs more than one off the rack. Just as many people prefer to have their clothes tailor-made—particularly if the standard sizes don't fit them—so you may decide that you need a rug of a unique size or shape, coloring or design. Although the process may be a lengthy one, it can be arranged.

First, decide on the measurements, coloring and approximate design of your "ideal" rug. If you have seen a rug with a design that you like, have it photographed so that both the overall design and the details can be clearly seen. If your model rug is handmade, photograph it from the back as well so that the design is even more delineated. If for some reason taking photographs is out of the question, make careful sketches of the design, using a one-inch-to-one-foot scale. Graph paper makes this easier to do. Then make a note of the colors you want in your rug.

Once you are equipped with measurements, colors, photographs or sketches, all you have to do is find someone who can arrange to have your rug made. If you are friendly with the owner of a nearby oriental rug store then he is the person most likely to be able to help you. Alternatively, the buyer for the oriental rug department in a large store may be willing either to arrange things himself or to put you in contact with an importer of rugs. An importer is in constant touch with the Middle East and would know exactly how to get the job done. (If you try all these avenues and still can't find someone to weave your rug, write to me at B.C.M./F.O.M.A., London, W.C.1, U.K., and I will do my best to help you.)

Most custom-made rugs are woven in Pakistan. The weaving of rugs in large quantities is a relatively recent (1930) development there, so the people of Pakistan are more inclined to be open to new ideas. The weavers in Iran and Turkey tend to prefer their traditional sizes, colors and designs.

The cost of having a rug made varies with the complexity of your requirements. At the time of this writing, custom-made rugs woven in Pakistan cost between $100 and $175 per square foot. So a twelve-by-nine-foot (3.66 × 2.74 m.) rug may be $10,800 or as much as $18,900. These prices include the transportation from Pakistan and the 5.5 percent United States Customs duty levied on oriental rugs. The price should also include your retailer's profit margin.

Having a rug custom-made takes a long time, so be patient. Remember that a weaver takes two or three seconds to tie each knot and your rug will probably have about 300 of these knots in each square inch—the process will clearly be a lengthy one. Besides, speed is far less important in Eastern cultures than it is in Western ones. If you do decide to place an order, then be prepared to wait six months or longer for your rug.

One client of mine had to wait almost two years. She wanted a rug woven in a particular shade of pale green to match an antique tapestry of which she was very fond. I placed the order for her and the rug arrived just four months later. However, it was a vivid shade of pink. I complained and the workshop immediately agreed to start all over again. A few months later

The Kennedy/Johnson portrait rug.

I received a Telex that said that the new rug was completed and about to be shipped. That one never arrived. The ship had caught fire and its cargo was destroyed. The third rug was just the right color. However, by this time the weavers apparently had mislaid my instructions and had casually chosen to weave a different design. My fourth attempt to fill this order was successful. My client's custom-made rug and her antique tapestry are now living happily together in the sunshine of California. Unfortunately, this tale is not altogether unusual. Both you and your agent may need a great deal of perseverance before you get your perfect rug—but it can be done.

If you want a rug that is really unusual, you could have a custom-made portrait-rug. As you can see from the illustration of the President Kennedy rug, the likeness can be remarkable. This rug was woven in the town of Tabriz in Iran. It has over 500 knots per square inch, measures three feet, two inches by two feet, two inches (.97 × .66 m.) and cost $4,000. The likeness was done from a twelve-by-nine-inch (.31 × .23 m.) black-and-white photograph. The "Arabic" inscription woven around the border of the rug reads: "America wishes peace and good will to all nations of the world." The "Kennedy rug" is black and white, but colored portrait rugs can also be made. These are less succcessful because the weavers insist on using bright colors for the lips and eyes which appear harsh to our Western eyes. However, time and sunshine will soften the coloring. These

Local people also have their portraits woven, like this Kurdish girl. The fact that her eyebrows meet shows she was too young to be allowed to groom herself as a woman. The rug was made in Tabriz circa 1960.

softer colors are what give the antique portrait-rugs their pleasant effect. Persian portrait-rugs were very fashionable in the late nineteenth and early twentieth centuries. During that time, many historically famous political, military and royal figures, including Moses and Queen Victoria, had their faces done up in knots.

The town of Meshed in Iran has been producing custom-made rugs for centuries. The only restriction is that the colors and designs will always be those traditional to Meshed: deep pinks with navy blue, with an allover floral design or a medallion design. Of all the rugs in Meshed, the very special pieces are produced by just one family workshop. These rugs are extremely fine, with a *minimum* knot count of 600 (the rest of the rugs produced in the area of Meshed average 200 knots per square inch).

The workshop where these fine rugs are made contains only five looms. As I was being shown through the gloomy interior, I was surprised to see that all the weavers were middle-aged men. They sat quietly, three to a loom, working away at enormous carpets. The only light came from smelly kerosene lanterns. They used *tikhs* with hooked ends to tie the minute knots and their gnarled hands glided across the surface of the loom, selecting the wool, tying the knot and cutting the thread all in one fluid movement. The men worked in an atmosphere of grim concentration. They barely acknowledged the presence of the workshop owner and they completely ignored me. I was relieved to leave them at their looms and return to the sunny concrete yard. There, the owner of the workshop explained to me that these taciturn clever weavers produce the finest rugs in Iran today, with the sole exception of Isfahan.

The rugs from this workshop are avidly collected by wealthy Iranians. I say wealthy because the price of these unique pieces is $1,500 per square foot. A twelve-by-nine-foot (3.66 × 2.74 m.) rug, the smallest size that the workshop produces, would cost $162,000. The accepted custom is for the prospective buyer to pay for his rug while it is still on the loom. The money is divided into four equal payments, the first being paid as soon as the details of the coloring and design of the rug are agreed on. The subsequent payments are made as each third of the rug is completed. The reason for this, the workshop owner explained, is that when these enormous pieces were only two-thirds completed, the weavers would frequently demand that he triple their wages or they would not finish the rug. Because a weaver's technique can be as personal as his handwriting, a rug is seriously devalued if the weavers have to be changed. Consequently, in the town of Meshed the weavers at this workshop earn more than the policemen or the schoolteachers. Even if you cannot afford one of these rugs, you may see examples of them in the major rug collections of the Metropolitan Museum of Art in New York City, the Corcoran Gallery of Art and the Textile Museum in Washington, D.C., and the Los Angeles County Museum of Art.

MYTHS

More rugs have been destroyed by myths than by moths. The first myth is that old and apparently worn-out rugs are worthless.

In the 1940s, thousands of "old" oriental rugs were thrown out in favor of the fashionably new machine-made rugs and wall-to-wall carpeting. Sometimes, all that is needed is a good wash and some minor repairs. After they are cleaned and restored, these rugs may turn out to be quite valuable.

However, not every old oriental rug is worth a fortune. The rug may need months of expensive repair work or it may not have been a good piece to begin with. So, before you plan that holiday in Bermuda, or whatever, assess your old rug carefully according to the criteria in Chapter 9.

If you are collecting rugs for investment purposes, there are several other myths to watch out for. One is that oriental rugs are not made today, at least not fine ones. The weavers of Isfahan and Qum in Persia and Hereke in Turkey, to mention just three examples, would be angry and amazed to hear that the millions of tiny knots they tie each year don't exist. This myth is usually coupled with the one that says that only old rugs have investment potential. This is very misleading. A new rug that has been carefully selected and for which the right price has been paid can easily equal the investment value of an old piece. Friends of mine paid $1,500 for a twelve-by-nine-foot (3.66 × 2.74 m.) Saruk in 1972. They had it evaluated in 1979 for $10,000; this kind of investment gain is not unusual.

"You get what you pay for." This old adage is not always true when you are buying an oriental rug. Do be sure that you choose a reputable dealer. Go to one you have checked out through friends or other references. If they are trustworthy, dealers will soon dispel the myth that all oriental rugs cost a fortune. There are groups of rugs that are still reasonably priced, such as the nomadic Turkish and Persian pieces.

A complaint rather than a myth is that oriental rugs are "busy." Before I became involved with them, I admit I thought they were, too. At first sight, the detailed, intricate patterns may appear to be overcomplicated, but even if you object to busy designs in general, be prepared to change your mind about oriental rugs. As you become more familiar with their art form, you may find yourself becoming totally involved in their beautiful, complicated patterns.

A good way to introduce yourself to rugs might be to start with a Persian Kirman. Kirmans have a graceful, simple medallion set in the middle of an otherwise undecorated background. The pattern reappears only in the border of the rug so that it frames the central medallion. Also, Chinese rugs, both old and new, use relatively simple designs. (Again, if you are collecting for investment, stick with the old and antique Chinese pieces; the

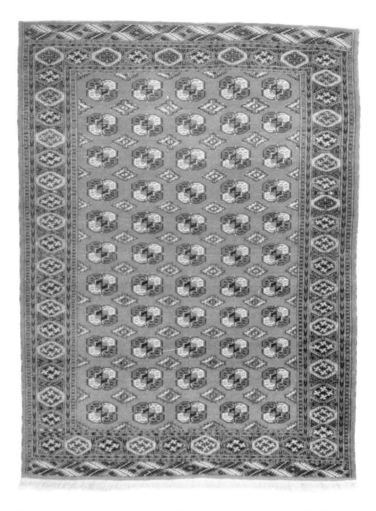

This Turkoman Bokhara design is copied in a wide variety of colors by the weavers in Pakistan, whose rugs are relatively inexpensive.

new, glamorous silk-washed rugs have little investment potential.) If you prefer rectilinear shapes you might consider the Bokharas or the Afghan rugs. The guls of these pieces will be drawn with varying degrees of intricacy, from the very basic designs of the Afghans to the more detailed patterns of the Turkoman region.

A plainly silly myth is that all "oriental design" rugs are genuine handmade orientals. This, of course, just isn't true. Remember that "oriental design" only means that the design came from the Orient; there are plenty of machine-made oriental rugs being produced in the Orient, too. So to be sure that the rug you are buying is a genuine handmade oriental, check that the design of the rug shows as clearly on the back as it does on the front and that there are small irregularities within the design. Another silly myth is that all oriental rugs are made in Persia. You now know that China, India, Turkey, Afghanistan and many other countries produce rugs that are called oriental as well.

You have only to visit your nearest rug store to see that the myth that all orientals are dark red and blue isn't true. The variety of colors in oriental rugs is really amazing and is part of what these rugs are all about. It is true that the weavers are very fond of red, probably because madder roots and ox blood are two of the most easily found dye stuffs. However, weavers have always been creative people and they work very hard to produce a rainbow of colorings. If you prefer to have a rug without red in it, you should be able to find one.

"The thicker the rug, the better (stronger) it is." These myths might apply to a machine-made carpet but they don't apply to oriental rugs. Orientals do not depend on thickness for their durability. If they did, then there would be no reason for the weaver to clip and, in some cases, shave away so much of the pile. The strength of an oriental rug comes from the quality of the materials used and the firmness and density of the knots. Rugs vary in thickness according to the area in which they are made. It is correct for some types of rugs, Bijars for instance, to be so thick that they are difficult to fold, but a silk Hereke rug of that thickness would be unthinkable.

The myth of "perfection" says that the only truly valuable oriental rugs are those completely free of imperfections. This is not so. Small imperfections in rugs are natural and acceptable. Because weaving is done entirely by hand, it is virtually impossible to make a rug as precisely as a machine can. The rug would also lack spontaneity and be very boring to live with. One of the imperfections most commonly found is the arbrush, the change of color that appears as a band across the rug. To oriental eyes, the rug may be of lesser value without an arbrush.

"Bokharas are the best." Perhaps the reason for this myth is that the name "Bokhara" has been given to such a wide variety of rugs. The fact is, some Bokharas are excellent and some are worth very little indeed.

A myth that I find strange is that good rugs have seven borders. It is true that some good rugs do have seven borders, but many more do not. Perhaps the myth came about because rugs with extremely detailed designs often do have many borders in order to balance their complicated central fields. Because rugs with intricate designs usually have a high knot count and will have taken longer to weave than the more simple pieces, they will be more expensive. But this has nothing to do with an exact number of borders.

"All good rugs are made by children." It is true that the majority of rugs with a knot count above 400 are made by children, although the fineness of the knotting does not in itself guarantee a "good" rug. Many wonderful rugs are produced by adults; their knotting may not be so fine but the workmanship often makes up for the fewer knots and can result in remarkably beautiful rugs.

A truly destructive myth is that oriental rugs can be cleaned only by beating them. The practice of hanging a rug over a clothesline and hitting the back of it with a stick or broom is prevalent in Southern Europe and unfortunately has found its way to America. Please don't beat your rug: beating it will break the warp threads and dislodge not only the dust but the weft threads as well.

One final myth: "An oriental rug will last forever." Providing you have chosen the right rug for your needs and are treating it properly with tender loving care, this myth, as you will discover, approaches reality.

GLOSSARY

Abadeh (AB-ah-day). Strongly woven, brightly colored Persian rug with small detached rectilinear figural designs, stylized tree of life, and diamond-shaped medallion.

Abrisham (AB-ree-sham). Persian silk.

Afshar (AF-shar). Persian nomadic tribe. Gaily colored woolen rug, typically blue, ivory, and red, with rectilinear designs.

Agra (AG-rah). Town in India, location of the Taj Mahal, and a prodigious weaving center.

Allover. Design featuring an allover, repeating pattern.

Altai Rug (AL-tay). Oldest surviving rug, dating from approximately 500 B.C.; also known as the Pazyryk Carpet.

Anatolia. Region of Turkey, best known for prayer rugs.

Arabesque. Design of curving tendrils.

Arbrush (AR-brush). Striped variation in tone of a color, appearing as a band across the face of a rug. Also *abrasch,* "*hairbrush.*"

Ardebil Rugs (AR-de-bil). Famous Persian carpets, made approximately 1540. Ardebil now produces softly colored, rectilinear-design rugs.

Armenia. Now a region in the USSR; produces well-made Caucasian-style rugs.

Aubusson (OH-byu-sohn). French rug with a flat tapestry weave; workshop established approximately 1743.

Baff. Knot.

Baluchi (bah-LOO-chee). Nomadic tribes of Turkoman, Afghan, and Persian border areas. Baluchi rugs, typically dark blue and rust red with rectilinear designs, often have highly decorated kelim ends. Also *Balouchi, Beloutchi.*

Berber. Moroccan "tribal" rug.

Bergama (ber-GAH-mah). Established Turkish weaving center.

Bijar (BEE-jar). Established Persian weaving center, producer of thick, strongly made rugs. Also *Bidjar.*

Bokhara (bo-KHAR-ah). Chief city of Turkoman region; also, the name given to the gul designs typical of Turkoman rugs.

Boteh (BO-tay). Persian "paisley"-type design.

Boteh-miri. A small boteh.

Candy. Side cord of a rug.

Catechu (CAT-ah-choo). Dye stuff used to obtain the color brown. Also *cutch.*

Caucasus. Region in the USSR; produces geometric-patterned rugs.

Charpay (CHAR-pay). Term meaning approximately four feet (1.22 m.) long.

Chosroes, Spring Carpet of. Famous sixth-century Persian rug.

Daftun (DAF-toon). Comblike tool used to hammer down weft threads.

Dhurri (DAR-ree). Indian version of kelim. Also *dhurrie, durrie.*

Dis-torba (dis-TOR-bah). Small bag, often used to carry salt and other household articles.

Doruye (DOR-ru). Reversible rugs with a completely different design on each side.

Dozar (DO-zar). Two zars (see *zar*), approximately two yards (1.83 m.).

Dragon-lung (dragon-loong). Chinese dragon symbol, male, sometimes called Lord of the East.

Feng-huang (feng-huong). Chinese dragon-phoenix, female, symbolizing opposite attributes from Dragon-lung.

Fo (fwo). The maned lion, a Chinese Buddhist symbol.

Fu (foo). Chinese bat symbol meaning luck and happiness.

Fu-ts'ang-lung (foo-t'song-loong). Chinese dragon symbol, guardian of treasure.

Gaichi (GAY-chee). Scissors used to trim yarn ends.

Ghashoghdoun (GHAS-OGH-doon). Small bag, used to store clothing and other household articles.

Ghiordes (YOR-dez). Turkish double knot. Town in Turkey known for prayer rugs, the best of them finely knotted with a short pile, rectilinear designs, mihrabs typically in a single color (never yellow).

Gul (goohl). Literally, "flower"; an octagonal design, also called "elephant's footprint."

Gulestan (GOOHL-es-tan). Prefix meaning "rose garden."

Gul-henna (goohl-hen-AY). "Henna blossom"; a motif often used in allover designs on Persian Veremin rugs.

Hamadan (HAM-ah-dan). Persian town, trading point for villages of Hamadan region.

Haroun (hah-ROON). Persian village near Kashan; also, a prefix frequently used at auctions to mean "coarse" or "poor quality."

Hatchlu (HATCH-loo). Large cross design (literally, "marked with a cross"). Also *hatchli, hatchly, hatschlou.*

Herat (heh-RAT). Town in Afghanistan, major collecting point for rugs of the Baluchi tribes.

Herati (heh-RAH-tee). Design thought to have originated in Herat, once capital of Afghanistan; it is often used in allover patterns.

Hereke (heh-ree-KAY). Town in Turkey known for extremely fine, close-clipped pure silk rugs.

Heriz (heh-REEZ). Established Persian weaving center; produces rugs made of wool, or occasionally silk, with geometric designs. Also *Heris, Iris.*

Inely (IN-lee). Prefix meaning "good."

Ipek (IH-pek). Turkish word for silk.

Isfahan (ISS-fah-hahn). Capital city of Persia under the Safavid Dynasty. It now produces some of finest rugs in Iran.

Isparta. Town in Turkey, former ancient Greek city of Sparta.

Kaba (KA-bah). Prefix frequently used at auctions to mean "coarse"; not to be confused with *kaiba*, a designation of rug size.

Kaiba (KAI-bah). Caucasian term designating a specific rug size: four feet to four feet, eight inches wide by nine feet, four inches to ten feet, six inches long (1.22–1.42 × 2.84–3.2 m.).

Karabagh (kahr-ah-BAGH). Caucasian province, next to the Kasak region.

Karamani (kar-ah-MAH-nee). Province of Turkey; also, Turkish term for kelim.

Kar-haneh (kar-HAH-nay). Workshop, "factory."

Kasak (kah-ZACK). Region of the Caucasus. Also *Kazak, Kazakh.*

Kashan (kah-SHAHN). Persian town long famous for fine rugs.

Kashgai (kash-GAI). Famous Persian nomadic tribes. Finely woven, rug of springy, lustrous wool, with detailed rectilinear designs. Also *Kashkai, Gashqai, Quashqa'i.*

Kashmir. The Vale of Kashmir in India; it produces silk as well as wool rugs.

Kayseri (KAI-za-ree). Turkish town, now known for "art silk" rugs. Also *Kaysari, Cesarea, Kaisaria.*

Keley (KEL-ly). Literally, "head"; a rug about eight feet, six inches by five feet (2.59 × 1.52 m.). Also *kelie, kelei, ghali.*

Kelim (kil-LEEM). Flat-woven ends of rugs; also, any piece woven without a pile. Also *kilim, gelim, ghilim.*

Kenareh (ken-ah-RAY). Literally, "side"; wide runner. Also *kenare.*

Kermes (KER-mez). Persian word for cochineal insect; also means "red" or "crimson."

Khorasan (KHOR-ah-san). Established Persian weaving center. Also *Korassan.*

Kirman (KER-man). Established Persian weaving center. Also *Kermann*

Kirman Laver (lah-VAHR). True Kirman Laver rugs are no longer produced; modern so-called Kirman Lavers are similar in weave to Kirmans, but their floral designs are far more intricate.

Konya (KOHN-yah). Town in Turkey known for kelims.

Kurk (koork). Finest grade of wool.

Mamluk. Egyptian rugs of the fifteenth and sixteenth centuries, named after the ruling dynasty.

Medallion. Circular or oval design, used as central motif.

Meshed (meh-SHED). Persian city. Strong, well-made rug with floral designs, deep pinks typical; sometimes called Isfahan Meshed.

Mianeh (mee-AN-ay). Literally, "the half"; a term usually used to denote size.

Mihrab (MEHR-ab). Arch design of prayer rugs; specifically, the top of the arch. Also *mirab.*

Milas (MEE-las). Town in Turkey. Turkisk prayer rug, usually wool, ground color typically terra-cotta mihrab often decorated with flowering tree of life, yellow frequently used as background for main border. Also *Milis, Melas.*

Mir (meer). Persian rug with repeating pattern of palm-leaf motif; also called Seraband Mir, after village of Mirabad in Seraband district.

Mira (MIR-ah). Palm-leaf motif. Also *miri.*

Mirzapur (MIRZ-ah-poor). Town in India known for inexpensive fluffy white rugs that may be of poor quality.

Mori (MWAH-ree). Term frequently used at auctions to disguise the fact that a rug comes from Pakistan; correctly used, a town in Afghanistan producing some of that country's finest rugs.

Moutesham Kashan (moo-tay-shahm). Antique variety of Kashan rugs. Also *Motasham, Motapashan, Mouchtaschemi.*

Mud (mood). Strong, finely woven, colorful geometric-design rug made in the Khorasan region. Also *muhd, mood.*

Mudjur (mood-jah). Turkish prayer rug, typically of wool, with deep red ground, design highlighted by clear forest green, blue, and bright yellows.

Muh (moo). Goat hair.

Nain (nai-een). Persian village known for the fine-quality rugs.

Nil (neel). Persian word for indigo.

Nim (neem). "Half"; e.g., *zaranim* = one and a half zars.

Palas (pah-las). Another name for kelims.

Pambe (pam-beh). Persian word for cotton.

Pamuk (pam-ook). Turkish word for cotton.

Pillar rug. Chinese rug made to be folded around a pillar so that the two long sides come together and the serpent or dragon typically decorating it appears to encircle the pillar. If borders are included in the design, they appear only on the short end.

Policheh (pol-lee-chay). Rug about seven feet by 4 feet (2.13 × 1.22 m.); i.e., a "standard-size" rug.

Polonaise (pol-oh-naze). Type of rug made in Isfahan, Persia, and so named because such rugs were commissioned by great Polish families.

Pushti (push-tee). Literally, "back"; the smallest-size rug, three feet by two feet (.91 × .61 m.).

Qum (ghoom). Persian Holy City, famous for silk rugs. Also *Kum, Ghum, Ghom, Qoom.*

Rutakali (roo-ta-cal-ay). A horse blanket.

Salor (say-lor). A major seminomadic tribe of the Turkoman region.

Saph (sahf). Design of Turkish prayer rugs, characterized by multiple mihrabs. Also *Sarph, Saaph.*

Saruk (sah-rouk). Established Persian weaving center. A richly colored, densely woven woolen rug, motifs usually floral, occasionally rectilinear. Also *Sarouk.*

Savonnerie (sah-vohn-nah-ree). French "oriental" rug with a cut pile; workshop established 1627.

Senneh (sen-nay). Persian single knot. Town in Persia that produces rugs with incredibly finely woven small floral designs (miniature version of Herati design is typical).

Seraband (sar-ah-band). Region in Persia; common name for an allover boteh design. Also *Serabend.*

Serapi. Another name for Heriz rugs.

Shah Abbas. One of Persia's most important rulers; also, a sweeping floral design named after him.

Shen-lung (shen-loong). Chinese spirit dragon.

Shirvan (shur-van). Region in the Caucasus.

Sinkiang (sin-kai-ang; shin-jiang). Province of China. The new varieties of Sinkiang rugs are brightly colored with geometric designs, and are also known as Samarkands after the town used as trading post. Old Samarkands are similar to antique Chinese pieces.

Soumak (soo-mack). Plant used to obtain mauve-blue color; also, a type of flat-woven rug, differing from kelim weaving in that the back is left unfinished so that loose ends of threads are clearly seen. Also *sumac, sumack, sumakh.*

Suf (soof). Persian word for embossed.

Taba-Tabriz. A latter-day variety of Tabriz rug; also known as Taba-Tabai.

Tabachi (tah-BAH-chee). Poorest-quality wool, taken from dead animals. Also *tabichi.*

Tabriz (ta-BRIHZ). Persian city. Rugs of quality levels are produced here, but the finest pieces equal Isfahans.

Tekke (TEK-key). A major seminomadic tribe of the Turkoman region.

T'ien-lung (tien-loong). Chinese sky dragon.

Tikh (TEE-kay). Knife with hooked end used to aid knotting.

Ti-lung (DEE-loong). Chinese earth dragon.

Tobreh (TO-bray). Small hammock-shaped bags.

Torbas (TOR-bahs). Pocketlike bags, often worn as saddlebags by goats.

Turkoman. Region in the USSR.

Ushak (OOH-shak). Turkish city in Anatolia. Also *Oushak, Yaprak.*

Verdose (FER-dos). Persian town known for rugs made from undyed wool, of coarse to medium weave, with geometric designs.

Veremin (VER-ah-min). Persian rug made from lustrous wool in rich colors, decorated with small flower and leaf designs in an allover pattern.

Yallahmeh (YAH-lah-may). Brightly colored, geometric-design rug made in the area of Aliabad near Isfahan; reminiscent of Kashgai rugs. Also *Yalameh.*

Yin-Yang (yin-yahng). Chinese symbol representing opposites.

Yomud (yoh-MOOD). A major seminomadic tribe of the Turkoman region. Also *Yamout.*

Zar (zahr). Approximately one yard (.91 m.).

Zaranim (ZAHR-ah-neem). One and a half zars. Also *sarenim.*

USEFUL ADDRESSES

Rugstop (mentioned in Chapter 6) is available from Doris Leslie Blau, Inc., 15 East 57th Street, New York, New York 10022. 212-759-3715.

National Association of Rug Cleaners (a division of AIDS International), 2009 North 14th Street, Arlington, Virginia 22201. 703-524-8120.

American Society of Interior Designers, 730 Fifth Avenue, New York, New York 10019. 212-586-7111.

If you wish to contact the author, please write care of B.C.M./F.O.M.A., London, W.C.1, England.

SELECTED BIBLIOGRAPHY

A. Cecil Edwards. *The Persian Carpet*. Rev. ed. Atlantic Highlands, New Jersey: Humanities Press, 1975.

Reinhard G. Hubel. *The Book of Carpets*. New York: Praeger, 1970.

Mohamed Seyed Ghaleh. *The Romance of Persian Carpets*. 10 vols. Celle, West Germany: Cyrus-Verlag.

Ian Bennett. *The Country Life Book of Rugs and Carpets of the World*. Plainfield, New Jersey: Textile Book Service.

Arthur Gregorian. *Oriental Rugs and the Stories They Tell*. New York: Scribner, 1978.

Preben Liebetrau. *Oriental Rugs in Colour*. London: Collier-Macmillan, 1963.

Ulrich Schurmann. *Caucasian Rugs*. Washington, D.C.: Textile Museum.

H. A. Lorentz. *A View of Chinese Rugs from the Seventeenth to the Twentieth Century*. London and Boston: Routledge & Kegan Paul, 1972.

Yanni Petsopoulos. *Kelims*. New York: Rizzoli Publications, 1979.

J. Housego. *Tribal Rugs*. London: Scorpion, 1978.

Siawosch Azadi. *Turkoman Carpets and the Ethnographic Significance of Their Ornaments*. London: Crosby Press, 1975.

J. Iten-Maritz. *Turkish Carpets*. New York: Kodansha International, 1977.

Malcolm Craig. *Successful Investment*. London: Allen & Unwin, 1979.

INDEX

About the Author

Caroline Bosly is the only woman broker to the international wholesale oriental rug market, situated in London. She was appointed by the British government's Central Office of Information to represent Britain in this field. Also a lecturer on oriental rugs, she has made frequent television appearances. Articles about her have appeared in *The Financial Times, The Daily Mail, The Observer, The Baltimore Herald, Vogue, The Investors' Magazine, Woman's Day,* and other international magazines.